JAMES

NCCS | New Covenant Commentary Series

The New Covenant Commentary Series (NCCS) is designed for ministers and students who require a commentary that interacts with the text and context of each New Testament book and pays specific attention to the impact of the text upon the faith and praxis of contemporary faith communities.

The NCCS has a number of distinguishing features. First, the contributors come from a diverse array of backgrounds in regards to their Christian denominations and countries of origin. Unlike many commentary series that tout themselves as international the NCCS can truly boast of a genuinely international cast of contributors with authors drawn from every continent of the world (except Antarctica) including countries such as the United States, Australia, the United Kingdom, Kenya, India, Singapore, and Korea. We intend the NCCS to engage in the task of biblical interpretation and theological reflection from the perspective of the global church. Second, the volumes in this series are not verse-by-verse commentaries, but they focus on larger units of text in order to explicate and interpret the story in the text as opposed to some often atomistic approaches. Third, a further aim of these volumes is to provide an occasion for authors to reflect on how the New Testament impacts the life, faith, ministry, and witness of the New Covenant Community today. This occurs periodically under the heading of "Fusing the Horizons and Forming the Community." Here authors provide windows into community formation (how the text shapes the mission and character of the believing community) and ministerial formation (how the text shapes the ministry of Christian leaders).

It is our hope that these volumes will represent serious engagements with the New Testament writings, done in the context of faith, in service of the church, and for the glorification of God.

Series Editors:
Michael F. Bird (Ridley College, Parkville, VIC, Australia)
Craig Keener (Asbury Theological Seminary, Wilmore, KY, USA)

Titles in this series:
Mark Kim Huat Tan
Luke Diane Chen
John Jey J. Kanagaraj
Acts Youngmo Cho and Hyung Dae Park
Romans Craig Keener
1 Corinthians B. J. Oropeza
Galatians Jarvis J. Williams
Ephesians Lynn Cohick
Philippians Linda L. Belleville
Colossians and Philemon Michael F. Bird
1–2 Thessalonians Nijay K. Gupta
1 Timothy Aída Besançon-Spencer
2 Timothy and Titus Aída Besançon-Spencer
James Ruth Anne Reese
The Epistle of John Samuel M. Ngewa
Jude and 2 Peter Andrew Mbuvi
Revelation Gordon Fee

Forthcoming titles:
Matthew Catherine Sider-Hamilton
2 Corinthians J. Ayodeji Adewuya
Hebrews Cynthia Long Westfall
1 Peter Sean du Toit

JAMES
A New Covenant Commentary

Ruth Anne Reese

CASCADE *Books* • Eugene, Oregon

JAMES

New Covenant Commentary Series

Copyright © 2024 Ruth Anne Reese. All rights reserved. Except for brief quotations in critical publications or reviews, no part of this book may be reproduced in any manner without prior written permission from the publisher. Write: Permissions, Wipf and Stock Publishers, 199 W. 8th Ave., Suite 3, Eugene, OR 97401.

Cascade Books
An Imprint of Wipf and Stock Publishers
199 W. 8th Ave., Suite 3
Eugene, OR 97401

www.wipfandstock.com

PAPERBACK ISBN: 978-1-7252-5532-6
HARDCOVER ISBN: 978-1-7252-5533-3
EBOOK ISBN: 978-1-7252-5534-0

Cataloguing-in-Publication data:

Names: Reese, Ruth Anne [author].

Title: James / by Ruth Anne Reese.

Description: Eugene, OR: Cascade Books, 2024 | Series: New Covenant Commentary Series | Includes bibliographical references and index.

Identifiers: ISBN 978-1-7252-5532-6 (paperback) | ISBN 978-1-7252-5533-3 (hardcover) | ISBN 978-1-7252-5534-0 (ebook)

Subjects: LCSH: Bible.—James—Commentaries. | Commentaries.

Classification: BS2785.3 R44 2024 (paperback) | BS2785.3 (ebook)

VERSION NUMBER 12/02/24

All Scripture quotations, except for James for which I have supplied my own translation, are from New Revised Standard Version Bible, copyright © 1989 National Council of the Churches of Christ in the United States of America. Used by permission. All rights reserved worldwide.

For Apostles Anglican Church
and
Rev. F. Martin Gornik, retired

CONTENTS

Preface | xi

Abbreviations | xiii

Introduction | 1
    What Supports the Identification of the James Who Wrote This Letter with the James Known as the Brother of Jesus? | 2
    Who Was James? | 4
    Who Was the Epistle of James Written To? | 6
    What Was the Community like That James Addressed? | 7
    What Kind of a Book Is the Epistle of James? | 8
    What Are the Major Themes of James? | 9
    How Should James Be Broken up into Units for the Purpose of Study? | 11

Commentary | 12
    James's Greeting (James 1:1) | 12
    Wisdom for Life (James 1:2–18) | 14
        Enduring Trials Leads to Maturity (James 1:2–4) | 16
        Fusing the Horizons | 19
        God Gives Wisdom Generously to Those Who Ask with Faith (James 1:5–8) | 19
        Fusing the Horizons | 22
        Unexpected Reversal (James 1:9–11) | 23
        Fusing the Horizons | 25
        Trials, Temptation, and Sin (James 1:12–15) | 26

Fusing the Horizons | 30
God's Good Gift, Life Itself (James 1:16–18) | 32
    Fusing the Horizons | 36
Receive the Word; Do the Word (James 1:19–25) | 37
    Fusing the Horizons | 40
    Those Who Do the Word Receive Blessing (James 1:22–25) | 41
    Fusing the Horizons | 43
True Religion (James 1:26–27) | 45
    Fusing the Horizons | 47
Love Your Neighbor (James 2:1–13) | 49
    An Example of Favoritism (James 2:1–4) | 50
    God Chooses the Poor (James 2:5–7) | 52
    The Law of Love (James 2:8–13) | 58
    Fusing the Horizons | 62
The Synergy of Faith and Works (James 2:14–26) | 64
    Faith without Works is Dead (James 2:14–17) | 65
    Faith in the One God (James 2:18–19) | 70
    OT Examples Demonstrating Faith without Works is Dead (James 2:20–26) | 71
    Fusing the Horizons | 76
The Untamable Tongue Capable of Great Destruction (James 3:1–12) | 77
    Fusing the Horizons | 82
    Destructive Speech (James 3:6–12) | 83
    Fusing the Horizons | 87
The Wisdom from Above (James 3:13–18) | 89
    Fusing the Horizons | 94
Friend of the World or Enemy of God? (James 4:1–12) | 95
    Fusing the Horizons | 107
Denouncing Boasting and the Rich and Encouraging Patient Endurance (James 4:13—5:12) | 108
    Condemnation of Arrogant Merchants (James 4:13–17) | 109
    Fusing the Horizons | 111
    Condemnation of the Rich (James 5:1–6) | 112

      Fusing the Horizons | 117
      Patient Anticipation of the Lord's Return (James 5:7–12) | 118
      Integrity in Speech (James 5:12) | 125
      Fusing the Horizons | 128
  Instructions on Prayer (James 5:13–18) | 130
      Fusing the Horizons | 135
  Two Ways (James 5:19–20) | 137
      Fusing the Horizons | 139

Bibliography | 141

Author Index | 145

Scripture Index | 147

PREFACE

About three years ago, I was in conversation with an editor about writing a commentary, but I wasn't sure that the approach of that project was a good fit for me. So, I walked and thought and prayed, and it became clear to me that what I really wanted to do in the next season of my work was to delve into the book of James. In a follow up conversation, the editor offered me several different biblical books to work on, but James was not one of them. So I said no. It was just one week after that "no" that I received an unexpected invitation to write this commentary on James. I knew immediately that this was the next thing I was supposed to work on, and I said yes, with joy. One of the reasons I was so excited about saying "yes" to this project was because I knew this was going to be a book that would be written for all those friends and family who love God, treasure the church, and serve others, but who have never been to seminary. And, I also knew that this introductory commentary would be a benefit to those who are pastors and to intermediate level students.

As I have been writing this commentary, I have also taught the book of James at many different levels. I led a weekly Bible Study in my church, I taught a class for intermediate MDiv students, and I puzzled over this book with PhD students. Many of the questions that students asked in those settings found their way into this commentary, and the answers that we discovered made their way in too. In every context and at every level of education, James spoke to us. The book challenged us to see the two ways that are laid out before us: the way of wisdom and the way of foolishness. This wisdom reverberated for us through discussions about trials and temptations, wealth and poverty, teaching and speech, faith and works. And, as we looked closely, we had a vision of the God who gives good gifts, chooses the poor, lifts up the humble, and hears the prayers of his people. Our attention to the word that is implanted in us helped us to think about the practical

Preface

choices we make in order to be doers of that word. This commentary is not just a book about what the biblical text means but about how we might live out the ancient wisdom in our century. My hope for you who read this book is that you, too, might hear the wisdom of James and consider how it can be appropriated in your context.

I am grateful for my institution, Asbury Theological Seminary, which has long valued commitment to both faith and scholarship and has supported that commitment with generous sabbatical leaves. I am grateful for friends and family who supported me through prayer and encouragement, especially my parents, Rebecca Idestrom, and my Friday Night Fellowship. And most of all, I'm grateful for my church family, Apostles Anglican Church, which has encouraged me as a teacher for many, many years. It is a joy to live, worship, and serve among you. I'm especially grateful to the Tuesday Morning Bible Study, who walked with me through the book of James, and to The Little Church, including Rev. Pam Buck, who read through the commentary before it went to the publisher. And finally, to our now retired pastor, Rev. Martin Gornik, who entrusted his long-standing Tuesday Bible study to my teaching over several months and who has cheered me on as a teacher, thank you.

ABBREVIATIONS

Antiq.	Josephus, *Antiquities of the Jews*
BDAG	Bauer, Walter, Frederick W. Danker, William F. Arndt, and F. Wilbur Gingrich, *A Greek-English Lexicon of the New Testament and Other Early Christian Literature*
BDB	Brown, Francis, S. R. Driver, and Charles A. Briggs, *The Brown-Driver-Briggs Hebrew and English Lexicon*
Diss.	Epictetus, *Discourses*
Ep. Lucil	Seneca, *Epistle Lucilius*
ESV	English Standard Version
HE	Eusebius, *Historia Ecclesiastica*
Jos. *Wa*	Josephus, *The Jewish War*
KJV	King James Version
LXX	Septuagint
NASB	New American Standard Bible
NET	New English Translation
NETS	New English Translation of the Septuagint
NIV	New International Version
NRSV	New Revised Standard Version
TDNT	*Theological Dictionary of the New Testament*

JAMES COMMENTARY

Introduction

Recently, a friend at church told me she had a real struggle when she first started reading James. Some people she knew told her that they loved James because "it is *so* practical!" But when she read James, it seemed to contain an ethic of perfection that she knew she could never achieve. Her inability to live the perfect life required by the author of James made her hesitant to engage the book more deeply. After all, was it really possible to live a life without doubt or favoritism or poorly chosen words that lead to conflict with others, even other believers? Would she really be able to care for the poor, pray for and anoint the sick, and stop judging her brothers and sisters? As if that were not enough, James didn't talk about the topics her church told her were important: Jesus, salvation, or the cross. What was she to make of this book?

Even my seminary students can struggle to make sense of James. Most of them are deeply embedded in Paul's theology of salvation by grace alone through faith in Jesus Christ. This often means that when they are asked how to understand what James says about salvation, their first inclination is to describe a process that starts with confession and repentance and moves to belief. But James does not talk about such a process, even in relationship to faith. Instead, his focus is on action. As one person put it, "Less talk, more walk." How are my students to make sense of a book that never explicitly mentions repentance and that casts faith as deeply connected to action?

James

As I have led Bible studies at my church and talked to a variety of lay people about the book of James, over and over one of the big questions has always been, "How can I use this book for my spiritual growth?" or "How do James's instructions apply to us today?" The sections titled *Fusing the Horizons* seek to suggest answers to these crucial questions about the role of James today for both individuals and congregations who are seeking God's wisdom for faith and life amid a chaotic world. The words "fusing the horizons" are a way of talking about how the world of a first-century text can inform our contemporary church, world, and spiritual life.

The inclusion of the book of James in the canon is a reminder that God reaches out to humanity through different voices. One way to think about the canon is to see it as a 66-book choir singing God's song, not with one single note but in a complex interweaving of voices stretching across the centuries. When I was in high school, I played the double bass. Now, many years later, when I listen to orchestral music, I hear the basses playing particularly clearly. My own experience of playing that instrument enables me to hear its contribution. Similarly, some Christians may resonate more with one part of the canon over another. Yet, the music would not be the same if some of those canonical voices were missing. Taking time to study the voice of James opens yet another avenue to understanding who God is and our relationship with God. In order to listen well to the voice of James, it is important to know something about the person who wrote the letter and the audience it was addressed to.

What Supports the Identification of the James Who Wrote This Letter with the James Known as the Brother of Jesus?

First, we cannot prove beyond a shadow of a doubt that the Epistle of James was written by Jesus's half-brother. James was a popular name in the first century, and there are quite a few men named James mentioned in the New Testament:

James, the brother of Jesus (Matt 4:21;10:2; 17:1)

James, the brother of John and son of Zebedee, one of Jesus's apostles (Matt 13:55) who was martyred in 44 CE (Acts 12:2).

James the Less (or "Younger") (Mark 15:40)

James, son of Alphaeus (Matt 10:3)

James, the father of Judas, not Iscariot (Acts 1:13)

Introduction

Second, the main reasons given for identifying the James who wrote this letter as the brother of Jesus are (1) the use of the name James; (2) the lack of any other identifying marker; and (3) the prominent position of James the brother of Jesus in the early church. The letter is explicitly identified as being written by a person named "James." Among those named James in the early church, the half-brother of Jesus was the most well-known and had a known position of leadership within the early church. No further qualification of the name is offered. Luke Timothy Johnson describes it this way, "The simplicity and apparent modesty . . . of the author's self-designation as [servant], together with the total lack of other identifying features or protestations of authority, suggests a [James] sufficiently well-known so as to be . . . accepted as an authority by readers."[1] Because of this, the church has generally held that the epistle should be associated with the most famous James in the New Testament, the brother of Jesus.

Most commentators identify the name "James" in the epistle's opening as referring to the brother of Jesus. However, there are three opinions about the authenticity of the letter. First, some see this as a genuine, early book written by James the brother of Jesus. Second, some think that the book contains ideas that were taught by James which were then collected and put together by an editor sometime after his death. Third, another group of scholars argues that it was written by someone long after James's death using the name of James (a phenomenon known as pseudepigraphic authorship). Unfortunately, the book of James was not well known across the Roman world in the early centuries of Christianity. Because of this, there were some questions about its authenticity even in those early centuries. Ultimately, we find that James is included in the canon and that the early church came to affirm its authorship by James the brother of Jesus.

Those who argue that this is an authentic letter by James, Jesus's half-brother, must also argue for an early date since James was martyred in 62 CE. Arguments in favor of an early date and authorship by James include the following: the letter claims authorship by James; has a strong Jewish tone; and shows reliance on sayings of Jesus without explicit reliance upon the written Gospels. In addition, it does not show any signs of a developed movement with approved church structures and offices in place such as we see in later books.[2]

---

1. Johnson 1995: 93.

2. Two scholars who argue for authorship by James the brother of Jesus are Davids 1982; Moo 2000.

In contrast, those who argue for pseudonymous authorship can argue for a range of dates but usually assign a date between 80 and 120 CE. Arguments in favor of pseudonymous authorship include the lack of early reference to a writing by James in the early church. If a book was written early in the life of the church by James, the brother of the Lord, it is hard to explain why such a book goes unmentioned for 150 to 200 years.[3]

There are several scholars who propose a third solution to the problem of authorship. These scholars suggest that an editor from the late first or early second century made use of either oral or written material that originated with James and then shaped that material into the book we know. Those who argue for this position retain both the significant influence of Judaism and the ethical interests of James along with a book shaped in response to the Pauline mission with its emphasis on salvation by faith in Jesus Christ.[4]

In my own view, the arguments put forth by those who see this as an authentic book written by James the brother of Jesus are the strongest. They account for the Jewish flavor of the book and the lack of church hierarchy in the book. At the same time, the relationship between James and Paul that is described in the NT (cf. Acts 15; Gal 2:9–10) can explain the exploration of the relationship between faith and works that is so prominent in James 2. On the other hand, one must acknowledge that the identification of James as the brother of Jesus and a corresponding early date of authorship remains difficult to prove with finality. Despite the questions around authorship, the church has found this epistle profitable for growth in faith and action.

Who Was James?

James, the brother of Jesus, is only mentioned a few times in the New Testament. For example, when Jesus visits his hometown, he is identified as "the carpenter's son" and his brothers are named as James, Joseph, Simon, and Judas (Matt 13:55; cf. Mark 6:3). Jesus's family is present during his ministry, and, like the disciples in Matthew, Mark, and Luke, his family does not fully understand his message. Matthew tells the story of a time when Jesus's mother and brothers were wanting to speak to him (Matt 12:46–50). When Jesus heard that they were there, Jesus used it as an opportunity to

---

3. Examples of scholars who argue for pseudonymous authorship include Allison 2013; Dibelius 1975; Laws 1993.

4. Painter 2019: 244.

teach about the new family that is made up of those who do the will of God rather than those who are related by blood. While this could be taken as an implicit rebuke of them[5] and does portray them as "outsiders," it does not exclude them from participating in God's family as those who join with others in seeking to do God's will.[6] After the resurrection, Jesus's family, including both his mother and brothers, are full participants in the community of disciples (Acts 1:14). By the middle of Acts, James the brother of the Lord has become the leader of the Jerusalem church, and it was James who led the Jerusalem Council that sought to work out differences between Jewish and gentile believers (Acts 12:17; 15:1–35). Paul passes on a tradition that the Lord Jesus appeared to James after his resurrection (1 Cor 15:7), and many have understood that it was through this resurrection appearance that James came to have faith in Jesus as Lord and Messiah. Paul also identifies James as one of the three "pillars" of the church alongside Peter and John. These three leaders in Jerusalem recognized and affirmed the ministry that God had given to Paul (Gal 2:9). These fleeting references to James tell us very little about James beyond his relationship to Jesus and his leadership in the early church. However, both the Jewish historian Josephus and church tradition fill in more detail about this brother of the Lord.

Josephus, a Jewish historian who lived from 37 to 100 CE, mentions in passing that James was drug before the Sanhedrin and consequently condemned to be stoned (*Antiq.* 20:200). The church historian Eusebius (circa 260–339 CE) tells us more about James's life. He identifies him as the first bishop of the church in Jerusalem (*HE* 2.1.2–5) and indicates that he was especially known for his piety, which included continual prayer and worship of God (*HE* 2.23.4–19). He was called James the Just by those who acknowledged his outstanding virtue (*HE* 2.1.2–5, citing Clement). Eusebius also describes his martyrdom in 62 CE. In this account (*HE* 2.23.4–18), James is confronted by members of the scribes and Pharisees. These groups were afraid that all Jews would come to believe that Jesus was the promised Messiah, so they approached James and asked him to make the facts clear about Jesus. Their expectation was that he would speak in a way that discouraged people from following Jesus. However, when James began to speak from the parapet of the temple in Jerusalem, he declared that Jesus was the expected Messiah. The response from these groups was to throw him over the parapet and, when they found he was still alive, to stone him

5. Blomberg 1992: 209.
6. Painter 2004: 31.

and beat him with a club until he was dead. James began life as the physical brother of Jesus,[7] became part of the wider group of people who interacted with Jesus during his ministry, developed into a leader in the early Christian movement in Jerusalem, and suffered martyrdom for his faithfulness to the Lord Jesus Christ. If the epistle that bears his name reflects even some of his concerns as a church leader, we see a person bringing together the practice of faith—care for the widow, the orphan, and the poor—with the awareness of God as both the Creator and the Judge.

Who Was the Epistle of James Written To?

James is written to a broad, general audience. The letter of James is addressed to "the twelve tribes in the dispersion." The twelve tribes are a reference to the whole nation of Israel, and the dispersion is a reference to the scattered nature of those tribes. This scattering (also known as the Diaspora) began with the exile of the northern kingdom of Israel in 722 BCE, when they were captured by the Assyrians and resettled in other parts of the Assyrian empire. Most historians think that these northern tribes became assimilated to the people around them and were no longer identifiable as separate tribal groups. In 586 BCE the southern kingdom of Judah was sent into exile by the Babylonians. There was a remnant of people from all the tribes that were left behind in the land during the deportation. However, these two experiences of exile resulted in the dispersion or scattering of the majority of all twelve tribes. While some of those from the southern kingdom returned to Jerusalem around 538 BCE, many remained in Persia. Over time, Jews migrated throughout the Mediterranean as well as living in the area of the former Persian empire. The dispersion or exile began as God's punishment of Israel for their unfaithfulness, but by the first century it had become an entrenched reality of Jewish life: many Jews lived far beyond the borders of Israel.

So, if the northern tribes have been assimilated and the remainder of the Jewish people are scattered around the Mediterranean world, what does James mean when he addresses his letter to "the twelve tribes in the

---

7. In the early church fathers, there is some discussion about exactly how James was related to Jesus, but in the New Testament there is no hint that James was anything other than the natural brother of Jesus. Suggestions that James was either a stepbrother or cousin arose as the church developed the idea of the perpetual virginity of Mary. For further reading in this area, see Bauckham 2004.

Introduction

dispersion"? First, the use of "twelve tribes" envisions the restoration of Israel and the completeness of God's covenant and kingdom. We see examples of this in the New Testament. In Matt 19:28, "Jesus said to them, 'Truly I tell you, at the renewal of all things, when the Son of Man is seated on the throne of his glory, you who have followed me will also sit on twelve thrones, judging the twelve tribes of Israel.'" In other words, part of God's mending of the world is the gathering together of the twelve tribes. Rev 7:4–8 also envisions every tribe being gathered by God. When James writes to "the twelve tribes," he is envisioning God's restorative work. Second, this leaves open the question of whether the audience he is addressing are Jewish believers or gentile believers. If this book is written early, there is good reason to believe that the audience that James envisions is mainly Jewish believers, people who were steeped in the Torah and in the wisdom literature of Israel and who knew the teachings of Jesus. Such believers may have already formed their own communities or may have been part of synagogues where there was disagreement about Jesus and the claim that he was the Messiah.[8] James is certainly one of the most Jewish books of the New Testament in terms of its flavor, and if it is written in the early years of the church by James the half-brother of Jesus, then it can also be understood as being addressed to Jewish believers in the diaspora—whether as nearby as Syria or farther away.

What Was the Community like That James Addressed?

This is a hard question to answer. Even if we understand that James sent this letter from Jerusalem, it is expressly designated as a letter sent to scattered communities of Jews living around the Mediterranean. The circumstances of those who might receive such a letter would have varied from one place to another. We can, however, note experiences that were shared by Christians in the first century. The New Testament records outbreaks of persecution from the early days of the church. Acts 7 records the martyrdom of Stephen in the early years or months of the church. Others in the book of Acts faced imprisonment, beating, and various forms of opposition to their message, both in Jerusalem and in other communities around the Mediterranean. It would not be amiss to suppose that those who followed Jesus either encountered such persecution or knew of others who did.

---

8. Allison 2013: 43.

Other trials were faced by both believers and unbelievers alike. Life in the first century was difficult, precarious, and challenging. In a world that revolved around an agricultural economy, many families were one harvest away from disaster. In this world, extended kinship networks were a lifeline. Families worked together cooperatively for the sake of survival. And one's reputation as both an individual and as a member of a family were important aspects of life in the first century. Of all the values that drove society in the days of the Roman Empire, honor was the most significant. Honor could come through one's family, particularly if one was born into a high-status family such as the family of Caesar, the family of local rulers, or a priestly family. Honor could also be earned through one's actions (for example, great deeds in war, carrying out one's religious obligations, being a person of sharp wit in the marketplace, and through being a benefactor or patron). Both individuals and families wanted to avoid things that caused disgrace or shame in the ancient world and pursue those things that brought honor in the eyes of those closest to them.

The economic system of the Roman world was a mix of both markets, trade, and coinage along with benefaction and patronage. Wealth during this time period was concentrated in the hands of the elite with perhaps the top 2 or 3 percent being very wealthy and most people living around the subsistence level. Of course, some were better off, while not being as wealthy as the elite, and others were destitute. There was no "middle class" as we understand it in western democracies. This created a world in which relationships among family members, between peers, and between people of unequal status were crucial to survival and flourishing.

Concepts such as honor, kinship, and patronage are not values that are first and foremost in the minds of twenty-first-century westerners reading James. But this was the cultural world that the people of the first century inhabited. Honor, friendship and family, and economics were crucial to life in the first-century Mediterranean world. Familiarizing ourselves with the world of the first century helps us hear the book of James in a manner like the first audiences that heard James's letter.

What Kind of a Book Is the Epistle of James?

James is widely recognized as a book that consists of more than one genre. It is clearly a letter that bears all the required markers of an ancient Greek letter: identification of an author (James), an audience (the twelve tribes in

Introduction

the Diaspora), and a greeting (Jas 1:1). The identification of the audience as a group located in the diaspora points towards a "Diaspora Letter." Such letters were usually sent by a recognized authority from a central location. Often, such letters served both to console the recipients who were separated from their homeland and to encourage them to live faithfully in the location they found themselves.[9] But the actual content of such letters could be quite diverse. Despite the diversity of such letters, it is surprising that the letter of James, unlike Paul's letters, contains no clear delineation of a problem or a set of opponents and no explicit reference to the cross or the resurrection of Jesus. In light of these notable differences and in light of the actual content of the letter, scholars have suggested that the letter contains several additional genres including (1) a collection of teaching (the technical term for this is paraenesis); (2) a collection of Jewish wisdom; and (3) a community rule that outlines the ethics of life together.[10] In addition, there has occasionally been the suggestion that James is a sermon or bears resemblance to a speech.[11] These categories are not necessarily exclusive of each other. This letter clearly contains instructive material as well as a Jewish flavor and tone, and it is meant for community instruction. It is less clear that the book was originally a speech or sermon, but the wisdom of the book has been evident to many generations of readers. This wisdom is expressed using a variety of techniques including pithy sayings (aphorisms), vivid metaphors and analogies, and diatribe. Diatribe as an ancient genre involves creating an imaginary dialogue partner (e.g., "someone will say," Jas 2:19) with whom the author enters debate (e.g., on the topic of faith and works). It can also involve hyperbole combined with rhetorically persuasive speech. It was common for literary letters to make use of multiple forms to communicate the essence of the author's message.

What Are the Major Themes of James?

Throughout the book of James there are several topics that are dealt with repeatedly. These include faith and doubt; speech and prayer; anger and conflict; wisdom; care for the needy; and righteous living. But sometimes readers (and scholars!) want to be able to identify one central theme of a book. Many scholars have tried to suggest a single theme that organizes the

---

9. Verseput 2000: 101.
10. Verseput 2000: 109–10.
11. Witherington 2016: 323.

whole book of James. An attractive suggestion has been made by Patrick Hartin, who identifies perfection as the main theme of James. He writes, "The idea of wholeness or completeness, whereby a being remains true to its original constitution, is the fundamental understanding of the meaning of perfection in James"[12] In other words, he sees the whole book as oriented towards bringing the reader into alignment with true wisdom and thereby leading to the reader's wholeness. Another suggestion is put forward by Dan McCartney, who argues that genuine lived faith is the central theme. He writes, "I propose that the overall theme of James, the matter that occurs not just at the beginning and the end but throughout, and that drives the deep concerns of the whole letter, is that genuine faith in God must be evident in life . . . and that if one wishes to avoid false faith (i.e., hypocrisy), the 'faith said' must correspond to the 'life led.'"[13] McCartney points us towards the meeting of faith and action and the identification of genuine faith as the major theme of the letter. Both of these suggestions can be helpful for thinking about the major themes of James, but what is interesting is that James himself does not identify a particular theme as the central or organizing theme of the book. My own position is to identify James, as Richard Bauckham does, as a compendium of wisdom.[14] In a fascinating discussion, Scot McKnight also raises concerns about an overemphasis on a central theme when studying the book of James. His approach is to consider what the book says about God (theology) and practice (ethics). As we look at James, what we find is that James brings to our attention a God who gives generously and that these gifts include wisdom, care for the poor and marginalized, and life itself. Every chapter in James tells us something about who God is, and every chapter in James invites its readers to respond with action: taking care about their speech and attitude; attending to the needs of those who are vulnerable; promoting peace; and caring for the community of believers. As the commentary unfolds, I invite you to watch for the ways that James describes God and for the calls to action James issues to his readers.

---

12. Hartin 1999: 89.
13. McCartney 2009: 57.
14. Bauckham 1999: 108.

Introduction

How Should James Be Broken up into Units for the Purpose of Study?

James is a difficult book to outline because its major topics and themes are interwoven throughout the book. I encourage all those who wish to be a student of James to consider both the book as a whole and smaller units at both the sentence and paragraph level. Ancient manuscripts were written in continuous script with no divisions between words, sentences, or paragraphs. They also contained very little punctuation. This contributed to seeing biblical books as a whole. Today's Bibles help us find and study individual verses, but it is important to always pay attention to the way those verses connect with what comes before and after. Having said that, there are a few patterns that help us think about units within the book of James. The opening chapter introduces the major themes of James including such topics as wisdom, faith, prayer, wealth and poverty, right action, the use of the tongue, and care for those in need. The chapters that follow contain a series of short essays on those topics. Many of these essays are introduced with a question and conclude with a pithy saying (known as an aphorism). These pithy sayings are often both memorable and ambiguous. Their ambiguity invites the reader or listener to meditate on the saying and probe its deeper meaning. Noting the presence of a pithy saying can help us determine the end of a unit of study.

Commentary

James's Greeting (James 1:1)

James 1:1: James, a slave of God and of the Lord Jesus Christ, to the twelves tribes in the diaspora, greetings.[1]

The book of James begins with the standard form of a first-century letter. Just as contemporary Americans when they write letters put the address at the top followed by the words "Dear Mrs. Smith," so too the ancients had a standard way of writing letters. This standard letter writing strategy at minimum consisted of the identification of the author and the audience as well as a greeting. Here, James identifies himself in terms of his relationship to God and Jesus as a slave. Second, he identifies his audience as the twelve tribes in the diaspora. Third, he greets them. The identification of the author and audience along with sending greetings are the bare minimum of the standard letter form but do show that James is a letter (see the introduction for more on the genre of James).

James identifies himself as a slave of God and of Jesus Christ. In the ancient world slaves held the least honorable position in society. Their masters had the power of life and death over them and always expected obedient service. When James identifies himself as a slave of God, he places himself in a position of full obedience, humility, and service to God. He belongs to God and is owned by him. In the Old Testament, important leaders like Moses and David were each identified as a "servant/slave of God" (Neh 10:29; 1 Chr 17:7; when these verses were translated into Greek, the translators chose the same word, *doulos* or "slave, servant," that we find in James). The greatest leaders of Israel were God's servants, and leaders

---

1. The translation of James is my own. Other biblical references are to the NRSV unless otherwise noted.

of the New Testament church, such as Peter, Paul, and James, identified themselves in the same way (2 Pet 1:1; Rom 1:1). Leadership in the church is first a position of humility before God in which one's full allegiance and obedience is given to the God one serves.

James addresses "the twelve tribes in the diaspora." Addressing a group in this way marks the letter in three important ways. First, it indicates that this may be a literary letter. Other New Testament letters are clearly addressed to a specific group, such as the church in the city of Corinth, but this letter is addressed to a very broad group. Literary letters rather than personal letters were a common way of communicating important ideas to those within the author's circle—in this case, those who participated in the Jewish church. Second, it indicates that many different churches were being addressed and not just one church in one particular location. Because of this, the advice in the letter is broad and general rather than specific to one congregation or one person. Third, it indicates that there is a group that has been scattered. Those who live in the diaspora are those who do not live in their cultural home. In this sense, the letter of James provides insight about how to live wisely in the midst of a culture that does not share the same values as James's audience.

The greeting offered by James is a simple equivalent to our English "hello."

James

Wisdom for Life (James 1:2–18)

James 1:2–18: Consider it all joy, my brothers and sisters,[2] when you encounter various trials, (3) because you know that the testing of your faith brings about endurance. (4) Now, endurance must complete its work, so that you may be perfect and complete lacking in nothing. (5) Now, if anyone among you lacks wisdom, that one must ask God who gives to all openhandedly and without reproach, and it will be given to that one. (6) But that one must ask in faith without doubting; for the one who doubts is like a wave of the sea being driven and tossed by the wind. (7) For that person must not expect to receive anything from the Lord. (8) This one is doubleminded, unstable in all his [or her] ways.[3] And the humble brother must boast in his high position, (10) but the rich in his humble state because he will pass away like a flower of the grass. (11) For the sun rises with scorching heat and dries up the grass, and the flower of it falls off, and the beauty of its face is destroyed; thus, also, the rich in his pursuits will fade away. Blessed is the man[4] who endures trials because when he has been shown to be genuine, he will receive the crown of life which was promised to those who love him. (13) No one who is being tempted should say, "I am being tempted by God." For God is not able to be tempted by evil, and he tempts no one. (14) But each one is tempted when he is drug away and enticed by his own desire. (15) Then, desire when it has conceived gives birth to sin, and sin when it has been brought to term gives birth to death. Do not be

---

2. The Greek text uses the word "brothers," but in this context the word is inclusive of both men and women.

3. A more literal translation of the text would note the switch from *anthropos* ("human") to *anēr* ("man"). More literally, Jas 1:7–8 might be translated, "For that person must not expect that he or she will receive anything from the Lord. This one is a doubleminded man, unstable in all his ways." Luke Timothy Johnson in his chapter "Gender in the Letter of James: A Surprising Witness" 2004: 103–13 notes that James uses androcentric language throughout the book. At the same time, Johnson notes that examining the explicit gender language in James "leads to the conclusion that although James's language and focus are androcentric, his value system is one in which traits stereotypically associated with male patterns of aggressiveness and dominance are evil, while traits associated with stereotypical female patterns of passivity, patience and self-donation are good, even when expressed by males" (106). In my own translation, I have aimed for a gender inclusive translation where possible that points to the wisdom applicable to all members of the community.

4. The Greek switches from the generic "human" or "person" (*anthropos*) in v. 7 to the gender specific "man" (*anēr*) in vv. 8 and 12, but the text should be understood as applying to all individuals within the Christian community.

led astray, my beloved brothers and sisters. (17) Every good gift and every perfect gift is from above coming down from the Father of lights, in whom there is no variation or passing shadow. (18) By his will he gave birth to us by a word of truth in order that we may be a certain kind of first fruits of his creatures.

The beginning of the first major section of James opens with words of wisdom. It doesn't open with a thanksgiving, a prayer, or a blessing like many other New Testament letters. There is no description of one specific problem that the church is facing whether that is internal division such as 1 Corinthians or false teachers as in Galatians. Instead, James opens in a way that calls to mind other biblical wisdom books such as Proverbs or Sirach.[5] It begins with short pithy sayings tied together by repetition. These short sayings introduce many themes, like trials and temptation; endurance and patience; faith, doubt, and prayer; giving and receiving; and walking well in this life, that will be developed later in the book.

Many of these sayings contain wisdom that can be applied broadly to many circumstances in life. Some scholars have argued that James is addressing a particular kind of problem like persecution or poverty. But the audience that is addressed is envisioned as both large and geographically diverse—twelve tribes in the diaspora. A book that portrays its audience in such large terms is inviting the application of its wisdom in a variety of circumstances. Such circumstances may very well include persecution and poverty alongside other human experiences such as illness and injustice. Considering the audience, it is not surprising to find that James's wisdom can be understood and applied in a variety of locations and life circumstances.

One of the interesting things to note about this section of James is that it begins in Greek with the words "all joy." Placing these two words at the beginning draws attention to the emotion of joy. The remainder of this sentence and the section that it heads should be read through the lens of joy, the experience of gladness. These two words are immediately followed by the imperative "consider," which includes the meanings "think," "count," and "regard." Emotions are often mistakenly thought of as irrational experiences that happen to humans and are beyond human control, but here

---

5. Sirach is a wisdom book written around 180 BCE by a scribe named Ben Sira. The book is also known by the names Wisdom of Sirach, Ben Sira, or Ecclesiasticus. This book is included in the canon by Roman Catholic and Eastern Orthodox Christians while Protestant Christians identify it as part of the Apocrypha.

James points to a mental component of joy. Emotions have both a physical aspect (e.g., a feeling that is felt in the body) and a mental aspect (a cognitive component of the emotion) that occur together. In addition, emotions are directed towards something. Without the object they are directed towards, emotions are meaningless.[6] Joy is the emotion that James brings to the front when he addresses the audience, and the choice to choose joy sets the tone for the opening portion of the letter.

Enduring Trials Leads to Maturity (James 1:2–4)

James calls the audience, "my brothers and sisters." These may be both his brothers and sisters in the Christian faith as well as ethnic kin through their shared Jewish identity. James instructs his Jewish-Christian family to consider it all joy when they encounter various trials (*peirasmos*). There are some experiences where it is easy to experience joy. We might think of such occurrences as a wedding or the birth of a longed-for child as occasions where joy comes easily; although, even on these occasions, many may experience mixed emotions. But James's instructions relate to things that are very difficult to consider with joy. Most English translations here read "whenever you face trials" (NRSV). The Greek word here is *peirasmos*, a word that can be translated as either "trial" or "temptation." Greek has one word for the idea of both trials and temptations. James uses both the noun (1:2, 12) and the verb (1:13, 14) in the first chapter of James. Most scholars argue that the word has two meanings: (1) trials that happen to people and (2) temptations, but these two ideas may be more closely linked than we often think. There are a variety of external trials that are mentioned in this book, including poverty (1:9), sickness (5:14), and oppression (5:4). In addition, there are a variety of internal temptations that James mentions, including the temptation to blame God when one experiences trials or temptations (1:13), the temptation to boast in or trust in riches (1:10; 4:13–17), and the temptation to misuse one's speech (1:26; 3:5–6). In addition, some of the trials that are mentioned in James can easily lead to the temptations that are also described in James. There may be external trials like persecution or poverty that lead to the temptation to blame God or to curse other human beings. When humans encounter external trials, the temptation may be to despair or blame God (1:13), but James instructs the audience to count the trial as an opportunity for joy. One of the ways

6. Hockey 2019: 26.

Commentary

Christians resist the temptation to despair or blame is by choosing joy. In a short article, A. Bowden points to Thomas á Kempis as an example of someone who thought about why temptation could also be considered a reason for joy. He lists these four: "(1) Temptation shows a person more clearly ... his need for God ... (2) temptation shows people what they are capable of enduring ... (3) temptations ... can aid in humility ... [and] (4) temptations ... reveal one's true nature."[7] Both trials and temptations can be an opportunity to practice and experience joy.[8]

Accepting testing and trials with joy was a common admonition in both Jewish and Greco-Roman culture. Such tests were seen as a way to prove what type of person you were (Epictetus, *Diss.* 3.10.11) and responding with joy showed one's mastery over the situation (Seneca, *Ep. Lucil.* 123.3). In the first century, the Jewish historian Josephus describes the Essenes[9] as people who faced torture from the Romans during the war against the Jews. Despite the pain and suffering they endured, he writes, they "did not shed a tear; they smiled, knowing cheerfully they would receive their souls again" (Jos. *War* 2.8.10). A few decades later, the book of 2 Baruch instructs the righteous to rejoice in their suffering now while preparing their souls for their future reward (52:6–7). Other New Testament texts also encourage Christians to rejoice in the midst of testing or suffering (1 Pet 1:6). Like his Jewish and Greco-Roman counterparts, James gives a reason for responding to trials and temptations with joy. He indicates this should be done "because you know that the testing of your faith produces endurance." The word for "testing" (*dokimion*) in verse 3 is different from the word that means trial or temptation (*peirasmos*) in verse 2. The word "testing" in verse 3 is the way that the genuine nature of something was determined; it can describe a crucible. In the Old Testament this word is used to describe the process of refining metal. Psalm 12:6 compares the words of the Lord to silver that has been refined (tested) in a furnace. And Prov 27:21 describes testing as a crucible where metal is refined. But the closest reference may

---

7. Bowden 2014.

8. I note here that Davids 1984 sees the suffering they experience through the trials as the occasion for the "eschatological joy of those expecting the intervention of God in the end of the age" (67). Even if *dokimion* (testing) invokes the crucible, that is not used solely in an eschatological context. It seems to me that others in both the Jewish and Greek contexts saw joy as a current choice and not simply a future expectation.

9. The Essenes were a separatist group of Jews living near the Dead Sea who lived in community with one another sharing resources, participating in shared worship, and engaging in study. Their community at Qumran was destroyed by the Romans in 68 CE.

be from the book of Sirach written about two hundred years before James. Sirach writes, "Accept whatever befalls you, and in times of humiliation be patient. For gold is tested in the fire, and those found acceptable, in the furnace of humiliation" (2:4–5). In James, the testing of faith is a crucible where faith is refined in such a way that it leads to endurance. Endurance is the ability to bear up when faced with challenges and is connected to the ideas of patience, fortitude, steadfastness, and perseverance.[10] In contemporary terms, we might think of this as "grit." Endurance was a virtue that could be strengthened through suffering. So, Paul writes, "We also boast in our sufferings, knowing that suffering produces endurance, and endurance produces character" (Rom 5:3–4). Both Paul and James see endurance in faith as an important virtue that leads to the deepening of character. And in the case of James, the idea that faith that is tested brings about endurance is a reason to look on the trials and temptations that are encountered as a cause for joy.

James 1:4 continues by creating a chain that links the endurance of testing in verse 3 with the development of maturity and wholeness in verse 4. Enduring trials has a destination: maturity. The Greek adjective *teleios* is a favorite of James. He uses it five times, which is more than any other book in the Bible. This word can be translated in several ways: perfect, complete, or mature. Here in Jas 1:4, it is used twice: it describes the "perfect" work of endurance, and then it describes the "perfection" of those who practice endurance. The "perfect work" that is produced by endurance is the perfecting of the human character in the Christian.[11] James further describes this as being "perfect and complete." Together this depicts the Christian moving towards wholeness through the faithful endurance of trials or temptations. In the twenty-first century, the word "perfect" is used to mean flawless, but in the context of James and other New Testament books, "perfection" is about becoming more and more whole or complete. The person who has endured trials gains wholeness. They are not lacking in anything, most likely meaning they are not lacking in any virtue that is needed for a wise life. Patrick Hartin puts it this way, "The call to perfection that James makes is essentially a call to integrity."[12]

---

10. BDAG, 1039.
11. Davids 1982: 69.
12. Hartin 1999: 15.

Fusing the Horizons

Pheme Perkins rightly notes that in our contemporary western world the words "perfect" and "perfection" have come to be seen as an "oppressive expectation."[13] We have become much more comfortable with accepting ourselves and others as we are with no demands for growth or change. But James envisions a movement that begins when the Christian encounters a trial or temptation. That trial or temptation can become a crucible for one's faith, and it is the endurance of that trial or temptation that ultimately brings about an outcome of "perfection." Part of the trouble in our contemporary perspective is that we think of perfection as flawlessness, but in the culture of the first century, being perfect is more closely associated with wholeness, completeness, and ultimately maturity. It was commonly understood that enduring trials well was a means of developing character and growing in maturity. Indeed, even in contemporary culture we talk about the ways that humans grow through their responses to the challenges they face. James envisions a person who endures the trials that they face with joy. Choosing joy may seem counter-intuitive in the midst of trials or temptations, but choosing joy is a way of recognizing that enduring these trials and temptations can deepen one's faith and grow one's character even if it is hard and messy along the way.

God Gives Wisdom Generously to Those Who Ask with Faith

James makes his insights memorable and catchy by repeating the same word or using words that sound like each other to link one saying to the next. This began in verse 2, where *chara*, "joy," plays off the word *chairein*, "rejoice/greetings," from verse 1. This pattern continues with the repetition of endurance, which links verse 3 to verse 4. The pattern continues again in verse 5, where James reuses the word "lacking" from the end of verse 4. Each repetition builds on or refines the thought that came before it. In James 1:4 those who are characterized as being whole are also identified as those who are *not lacking* in anything. In Jas 1:5, anyone who *lacks* wisdom is to ask. Their prayer is to be directed to God, who is described as one who gives to all with an open hand.

In order to ask God for wisdom one must identify a shortage of wisdom. Indeed, the experience of trials and temptations may make one more

---

13. Perkins 1995: 97.

readily aware of the insufficiency of the wisdom one already possesses. In verse 4 enduring trials and temptations leads towards maturity, but even maturity or perfection does not mean that there is no room for further growth. For example, in the book of Hebrews, Jesus is described as learning obedience through suffering and being made perfect (Heb 5:8–9). In other words, even the Son of God, who was already whole, mature, and complete, could grow and learn, and this growth took place through suffering. Likewise, even those who endure trials and temptations with joy, knowing that this helps them become mature, can still recognize their need for greater wisdom. When they do, they should ask for this wisdom from God, who is described as "the God who gives." Later in James, we will see that God is the one who gives every perfect gift (1:17) and that God is one who gives grace, especially to the humble (4:6). God is a giver of gifts.[14] One of the gifts that God gives is the gift of wisdom, a capacity to understand that enables the one who is wise to live well in accordance with the knowledge that is received. God gives this gift without reservation. God has a simple, straightforward, and open response to the one who asks. God does not mock, shame, revile, or demean the one who asks, nor does he use the giving of the gift of wisdom as a means of manipulating the receiver into doing something on God's behalf. James instructs his audience to ask and then indicates that they will receive the wisdom that they ask for.[15]

When Christians ask God for wisdom, their prayer is to be characterized by faith rather than by doubting. Faith is about trust. The Christian is invited to have confidence in the nature and character of God as one who gives open handedly. The Greek word *haplōs* often means "simply" and refers to something that is done in a pure and open way. Responding in faith to this characteristic of God invites the believer to trust God's good and pure intentions and purposes in granting wisdom to the one who asks. In contrast to this is the person who asks but who doubts. In broader Greek literature, both before and after the New Testament, the word *diakrinō* means "argue" or "dispute." In fact, during this time period, it is only in the New Testament that it is translated as "doubt."[16] This development in the meaning of the word draws on the idea of an internal dispute within the person. Its use in contexts that place it in a mutually incompatible relationship

---

14. For more on "Gifts in the First Century," see the commentary and the sidebar on Jas 1:17.

15. For more on wisdom, see the commentary on Jas 3:13–18.

16. BDAG, 231.

to faith (e.g., Mark 11:23) and early translations and uses of Jas 1:6 point to the meaning "doubt."[17] The contrast in Jas 1:6 is between a person who trusts God to give the wisdom that is requested and a person who wavers internally between two positions—trust and distrust. The doubter does not trust God's character or good intentions. Metaphorically, those who doubt are like a rough wave in the sea that is driven and tossed by the wind. The metaphor portrays the one who doubts as wavering and being controlled by forces beyond themselves. Throughout the book of James, the reader is presented with stark contrasts such as faith/doubt; poor/rich; friend of God/friend of the world. These contrasts are a feature of ancient wisdom literature and invite the hearer to think about and choose the better part of the pair. This feature of wisdom literature is known as "two ways theology." The audience is presented with two opposites in which one is clearly the better way. Here, the choice is between trust and doubt, and it is clear that trust is the better way. This two ways theology will show up repeatedly in James. Verse 7 goes on to indicate that the doubter must not expect to receive anything from the Lord. God is characterized as a pure and unreproachful giver, but God is not an indiscriminate giver. He gives to the person who trusts God's generous and willing nature to give the wisdom requested. The one who doubts does not receive from God. This person is further characterized in Jas 1:8 as being "double-minded." This unique word, *dipsuchos*, quite possibly coined by James, is not found in Greek texts prior to the letter of James. But it clearly refers to the double-minded person, an idea that is not new to Greek speakers. The doubter, the one who hesitates, is further described as unstable in all his ways. "Way" was often used to refer to the life path that one has chosen. For example, Ps 1:6 says, "For the Lord watches over the *way* of the righteous, but the *way* of the wicked will perish." Similarly, in Prov 4:11 the king tells his child, "I have taught you the *way* of wisdom; I have led you in the paths of uprightness." He then continues with a contrast, "Do not enter the path of the wicked, and do not walk in the *way* of evildoers" (Prov 4:14). These texts present a contrast between a way of life that is righteous and one that is evil. James, too, presents a contrast in these opening verses. The contrast is between a person who chooses wholeness or maturity or a person who is double-minded, an unstable doubter. James presents this simple contrast to his audience as a way of pressing them to choose. And each choice moves the

17. Allison 2013: 180–81.

person either closer to righteousness or closer to wickedness.[18] God is the giving God who gives wisdom to those who ask. In a world where gifts create obligation and where reciprocity is expected, those who doubt the giver are people who find themselves under dual obligations. On the one hand, they are obligated to the generous giver, and in another way, they are obligated to themselves, to a view of themselves as somehow not dependent upon God and his generosity.

Fusing the Horizons

From the beginning of Jas 1:5, it is clear that we are not self-sufficient individuals. Instead of thinking that we must know everything we need to know in order to live a wise life, Christians are invited to ask God for what they lack and especially to pray that God would give them wisdom. This asking is to be characterized by trust in God's character, nature, and activity rather than internal doubt and division. The whole book of James is characterized by contrasts. In these verses, the contrast is between faith and doubt, but in the rest of the chapter we will encounter other contrasts (rich and poor; hearers versus doers of the word). These dualities challenge us. How, after all, can we live in a way that trusts God and is free of doubt? Not only does this seem beyond our capacity or experience, it also is at odds with the way knowledge has developed since the Enlightenment. Moore-Keish in her commentary on James points out that our world is characterized by doubt and indeed much of our current knowledge is derived from thinkers like Descartes, who dared to doubt the accepted wisdom of various traditions handed down over the centuries. She then goes on to point out that James is concerned not with the production of knowledge but with our capacity to be people of wholeness, people who have the capacity for an undivided heart that trusts God.[19] Those who wish to pursue wholeness may need to repeatedly choose faith over doubt. For those who struggle with doubt, it can be helpful to remember two things. First, James is using the wisdom genre to encourage people to choose trust in God as strongly as they are able. Second, other parts of the canon show that Christians can ask Jesus to help them with their doubt or unbelief. Remember the story of the man who brought his son to Jesus for healing? "Jesus said . . . 'All things can be done for the one who believes.' Immediately the father of the child cried

---

18. Lockett, 2008: 80, drawing on Tollefson 1997: 62–69.
19. Moore-Keish 2019: 32–34.

Commentary

out, 'I believe; help my unbelief'" (Mark 9:23–24). For those who struggle with doubt, asking Jesus to help with that struggle is part of asking for God's wisdom.

Unexpected Reversal (James 1:9–11)

Having just talked about maturity, wisdom, faith, and doubt, James now turns his attention to another topic that is prominent in wisdom literature: humility (often linked with being poor) and riches. The person of humble circumstances is one who must trust God for daily provision, while the rich may be tempted to trust their wealth and doubt that they must depend on God each day. In the puzzling set of instructions that follow, the humble are to boast in their high position and the rich in their humble state. Early in James's book, the reader is reminded that outward appearances are not a reliable indicator of a person's true position. In fact, in a surprising reversal the humble and the rich find their circumstances and the object of their boasting flipped.

James has been talking to believers, people he calls "my brothers and sisters" (1:2). Now, he speaks to a particular brother or sister,[20] one who is humble or lowly, a person who lacks resources. He instructs that person to boast in his high position. While in the eyes of society this believer may be a person of humble means, his status as a believer, as one who trusts God, gives him a high position. This is not a position that he has earned but rather a status that comes about because of his relationship with God. In this context, to boast in his high position is to boast in what God has done on behalf of one who is lowly. Such boasting honors God as the one who has lifted up the lowly (see commentary on Jas 4:10 for more on humility and exaltation). In contrast, the rich are to boast in their humble state. Again, in the eyes of society, the person who is rich may be honored and respected because of their wealth. They are seen as being successful and having achieved a certain status because of their riches. But this person is told to boast in their humble estate. The rich person is reminded that "he

---

20. By identifying the one who boasts as a "brother," James draws attention to the family relationship of the humble one. This is a person who is a member of the family, most likely the family of believers (although some identify the family here as being of Jewish background). James has already drawn out the tribal identification of his audience—a group tied together by their shared ancestry. Now, the humble one is identified as one who belongs to the group, a brother. This "brother" is most likely representative of a group of humble poor who are part of the larger community of believers.

will pass away like a flower of the grass." The humble state of the rich person is the recognition that he is completely human and therefore subject to all the realities of finiteness. The rich cannot take their wealth with them to the afterlife. They cannot avoid death. Their life is temporary and short. Their wealth is temporary and transitory. In light of this, the rich must boast in his mortal humanity. What effect does this have on the rich person? The rich person who boasts in his lowliness does not think that his wealth is something that he has earned, that he deserves, or that should be used to give him greater status. The rich person who boasts well boasts in his lowly state as a human being. Similar condemnation of boasting in riches is found in the Old Testament. For example, Jer 9:23–24 says, "Do not let the wise boast in their wisdom, do not let the mighty boast in their might, *do not let the wealthy boast in their wealth*; but let those who boast boast in this, that they understand and know me, that I am the Lord; I act with steadfast love, justice, and righteousness in the earth, for in these things I delight, says the Lord" (emphasis added). James, as he does throughout his book, does not simply copy the wisdom of the Old Testament or even the wisdom of Jesus; instead, he makes it his own. In this case, readers are invited to contemplate what the humble position of the rich person might be as part of appropriating James's wisdom for themselves.

Many commentators raise the question of whether the rich person described in verse 10 is a believer. This is unclear from the Greek text. On the one hand, the word "brother" is not repeated in verse 10, and this may point to the rich person as someone who is not a believer and/or not a member of the community. This position is strengthened when one considers the negative portrayal of the rich in the rest of James. In Jas 2:6–7 the rich are described as people who lord it over James's readers ("you") and drag them into court. In Jas 5:1–6 the rich oppress the poor, steal from workers, and live a life of flagrant luxury. There is nowhere in James where the rich are portrayed positively. On the other hand, leaving out words in Greek is common (referred to as ellipsis), especially in the short pithy sayings that make up wisdom literature. Indeed verse 10 does not repeat the verb "boast" either. The verb "boast" in verse 9 governs both the humble brother (v. 9) and the rich (v. 10). For those reading the book for the first time, this opening introduction to the rich is neither effusively positive nor desperately negative. It is only as one reads further into the book that the negative portrayal of the rich becomes clear. Here, there is ambiguity. However, the rich person is told to boast in his humble position *because* he will pass away just like grass flowers pass away. The life of the rich person is ephemeral just like the flowers that form on grass. Most people never notice grass flowers because they are small and often look like seed pods rather than flowers. When they do bloom, the flowers are not showy and last just a few days. The rich person who boasts in his humble position is one who recognizes the transitory nature of his life and riches.

James concludes this little section on the lowly and the rich with a timeless reminder that alludes to Isaiah 40:6b–8, "All people are grass, their constancy is like the flower of the field. The grass withers, the flower fades, when the breath of the Lord blows upon it; surely the people are grass. The grass withers, the flower fades; but the word of our God will stand forever." Isaiah highlights both the transitory nature of humanity and the enduring reality of the word of God. In James, the reader is reminded that the sun rises and in the heat of the day the grass dries up. When the grass dries, the small flowers also dry up and fall off. Their productivity and potential for fruitfulness are destroyed. The beauty that is found in the face of the flower perishes. The saying hammers home the harsh reality that beauty and flourishing are temporary. Unlike Isaiah, in James there is no emphasis on God or on the eternal nature of God's word. Instead, there is a relentless focus on the fleeting and the short-lived. The author highlights the withering, falling, and perishing grass flowers. Those who are rich share in the same reality of life's brevity. While they may be tempted to think that their pursuits are of great importance, the truth is that they will fade away, disappear, or wither just as the grass and flowers do when the sun rises and the heat of the day comes. Indeed, death comes to everyone, whether rich or poor, but the rich, perhaps, have more capacity to deny their impending passing as they go about their daily pursuits.

Fusing the Horizons

Wealth continues to be a significant measure of status in the eyes of many. Those who have wealth are described as having "made it." Those who struggle with poverty are often seen as responsible for the difficulties they face. We interview people of high status—celebrities, billionaires, politicians—for their views and advice while ignoring the hard-won wisdom of those who live on the margins. James's reminder that life and riches are both transitory is just as true today as it was two millennia ago. Instead of boasting about money or trusting our security to well filled bank accounts, those with wealth are to remember the transitory nature of being human. Meanwhile, believers who experience poverty are not to share in the world's view of their position but rather to boast in the position they acquire through God and through their identification as members of the family of God. And, as in the first century, so too in the twenty-first century, neither the poor nor the rich are to brag about their status as rich or poor; rather, they are to brag about what God has done for them. In this way, the poor are lifted up and the wealthy are humbled—both find themselves ultimately dependent upon God rather than themselves. It is not just James who has this vision, for in the Gospel of Luke we also find this same great reversal (Luke 1:52–53; 6:20–21).[21]

Trials, Temptation, and Sin (James 1:12–15)

After exploring the contrast between the humble and the rich, James returns to the theme of trials, temptation, and testing that began in verses 2–3. If you read a variety of English translations of Jas 1:12, you'll find that they are split between versions of "blessed is the one who endures *trials*"[22] and "blessed is the one who endures *temptations*."[23] As discussed earlier in the commentary, this is because Greek only has one word that covers the concepts of trial and temptation. James 1:2–4 has already shown us that joy is an appropriate response to trials or temptations because it is an opportunity to persevere and grow in one's endurance, and faithful endurance leads to wholeness. Now, James also uses a beatitude to indicate that enduring trials leads to blessing. Blessing is associated with being fortunate or receiving privilege from God. In the first century, this kind of privilege is associated with honor and high status, which was a key cultural value of the time. When James says "blessed," we might hear him saying, "How honorable!"[24] This theme of honor continues with the outcome of enduring trials. Those who endure trials are identified as being "genuine" or "approved." The language of genuineness was often associated with coins in the first century to

---

21. For more on the poor and rich in James, see the commentary on Jas 2:1–13; 4:13–27; and 5:1–6.

22. ESV, NIV, NJB, RSV.

23. KJV, NRSV. The NLT tries to capture both with "God blesses those who patiently endure testing and temptation."

24. Hanson 1994: 81.

describe their authenticity and worth.[25] Those of high value were honored. The person who endures trials well affirms the authenticity and value of their faith, a faith that leads through endurance to wholeness. The person who endures also receives "the crown of life." Crowns were an important symbol of honor in the ancient world.[26] Those who had achieved significant accomplishments were recognized with crowns, some made of gold others made of flowers or leaves. Those who received crowns made from imperishable materials might wear them at civic events, and the crowns were a mark of the honor they had received. In James, the crown is given to people who endure trials in a way that reflects their faith in God. This person will receive "the crown of life." This refers to the gift of eternal life given to those who with faith in God persevere through trials and temptations to the end. The gift of eternal life is a gift that begins now in relationship with God and continues into eternity. From the beginning of this letter there have been hints that James is written in a context where there is an awareness of the future and the last days.[27] "In 1:2–4, refining faith by trials is a recurrent eschatological theme (cf. Isa 4:3–4; Mal 3:1–5; Zech 13:9). In 1:9–11, there is an eschatological reversal of fortunes. In 1:12, there is a reward for those who remain steadfast in the midst of trials."[28] Each of these themes points to the end times horizon that informs James's wisdom about how to live in the midst of current trials and temptations. The world does not simply go on forever; instead, Christians anticipate the return of Christ and a time when everything will be set right in this world. Understanding that end time horizon is a key part of James's wisdom for life. The person who endures trials and temptations in this life will receive honor, recognition, and eternal life from God. But we should be careful to understand that the reward that those who endure trials receive is not simply eternal. It is also now. It is life itself but not a continuation of ordinary life; rather, it is a "good, lasting, eternal, different from the past" life.[29] For those whose trials include poverty and oppression, the message of James is particularly meaningful. Those who endure will receive not the judgment and oppression of this world but honor from the God who sees, gives wisdom, and grants reward to those who love him. "James's expression . . . identifies those who

---

25. Vlachos 2013: 39.
26. Wright 2023.
27. Scholars refer to the study of the last days or the end times as eschatology.
28. Morales 2018: 112.
29. Tamez 2002: 33.

endure the trial with those who love the Lord . . . Those who do not love the Lord do not endure the trial. The loving identification with the Lord strengthens hope and helps to overcome hostile situations. To love God is the other part of the 'royal law' that James summarizes in 2:8: 'You must love your neighbor as yourself.'"[30] Loving God is not simply about obedience or faithfulness but also about the affection for God that sustains the endurance of trials.

In verse 13 most English translations switch from the translation "trial" or "test" to the translation "tempted." Up until this point, James has used the noun that can mean either trial or temptation, but now he switches to the verb which can also mean either "to test" or "to tempt." There are a couple of reasons that translations move from testing to tempting. First, James does not want to associate God with evil in any way. However, we should note that in the Old Testament God does test people. For example, God tested Abraham to see if Abraham would demonstrate his trust in God by offering up his son Isaac on an altar (Gen 22:1–2). When Abraham completed that test, God both provided the ram to be offered on the altar and reconfirmed his covenant promises to Abraham (Gen 22:13–18). Second, the view that God (or the gods) were not associated with evil was shared by some Romans who also did not believe that human troubles were caused by the gods. "The idea that the gods are not responsible for evil was famously affirmed by Plato at the end of his *Republic*. . . . God, as Plato explains there, is not responsible for the evils that afflict humans; human beings themselves, since they are endowed with free will, choose their own kind of life and whether or not to adhere to virtue."[31] Because James removes God from any association with evil, translators move from the idea of "trial" in the first twelve verses of James to the idea of "temptation" in verses 13–15. James sees God as the creator who gives good gifts (v. 16) and not as a tempter (v. 13). When humans experience trials and temptations, they are not to blame God for those trials or temptations. James firmly locates temptation in the realm of human desire instead of attributing it to God. In addition, this segment (vv. 13–15) ends with a description of sin. In this context, shifting the translation to "tempting" fits the larger context of this segment. John Calvin explained the switch to temptation this way:

> *Let no man, when he is tempted.* Here, no doubt, he speaks of another kind of temptation. It is abundantly evident that the external

30. Tamez 2002: 33.
31. Ramelli 2009: 98.

> temptations, hitherto mentioned [vv. 2–12], are sent to us by God. In this way God tempted Abraham (Genesis 22:1) and daily tempts us, that is, he tries us as to what are we by laying before us an occasion by which our hearts are made known. But to draw out what is hid in our hearts is a far different thing from inwardly alluring our hearts by wicked lusts.
>
> He then treats here of inward temptations which are nothing else than the inordinate desires which entice to sin. He justly denies that God is the author of these, because they flow from the corruption of our nature.
>
> This warning is very necessary, for nothing is more common among men than to transfer to another the blame of the evils they commit; and they then especially seem to free themselves, when they ascribe it to God himself. This kind of evasion we constantly imitate, delivered down to us as it is from the first man.[32]

James makes it clear that God is in no way associated with evil. Instead, each individual person is tempted by their own evil desires. In a chain that goes from verse 14 to verse 15, James identifies a process that begins with temptation and leads through sin to death. The metaphors used in this progression highlight how one thing gives birth to another until the ultimate outcome is death.

Temptation begins with each person's desire. While the Greek word for desire is occasionally used in the New Testament with a positive sense (Phil 1:23; Luke 22:15; 1 Thess 2:17), it is far more often used to denote a "desire for something forbidden or simply inordinate."[33] In James, the person is drug or pulled out of a safe place by skewed desires. Thayer puts it this way, "The metaphor is taken from hunting and fishing: as game is lured from its covert, so [a human is lured] from the safety of self-restraint to sin."[34] The second metaphor is just as vivid. The person is enticed by his or her desires. The image is of desire as a baited hook thrown out to snare the fish. Then, one thing leads to another. "'Desire' is personified as a woman who lures the listener into a sexual encounter, giving birth to a child named 'sin,' who then bears a grandchild named 'death.'"[35] This vivid metaphor may allude to the seductress of Prov 5 and 7, where the listener is presented with a choice between the wisdom of avoiding temptation or giving in to

---

32. Calvin 1847 (emphasis original).
33. BDAG, 372.
34. Thayer, $εξελκω$, n.p.
35. Moore-Keish 2019: 54.

temptation. James is not solely concerned with the temptation of sexual sin but rather with the wide variety of desires that can lure the Christian into sin. James taps into an ancient image of the temptress. But in our contemporary interpretation, we should be careful not to blindly associate women with sexual sin and temptation. Martha Moore-Keish writes:

> The gendered description ... can reinforce negative stereotypes of women ... playing into the cultural assumption that women are more fickle ... than men. ... Those who work with James today need to exercise caution about simply passing on such embedded stereotypes of women as dangerous temptresses. ... This portrayal can damage women and undermine healthy relationships between women and men.[36]

It is desire that conceives, and that which is born from desire is sin. Later in James, sin will be specifically associated with discrimination against others (2:9) and with failing to do what is right (4:17). Scot McKnight writes that "James defines sin relationally—anything contrary to love of neighbor (2:8–9, 12–13)—and judicially—an infraction of the Torah (2:10–11)—but ultimately he defines it theologically—something out of tune with God's will (2:11)."[37] Temptation leads to sin and sin when it has come to term brings death. This chain is an allusion to the story of the first human sin in Genesis 3, where Eve "saw that the tree was good for food, and that it was a delight to the eyes, and that the tree was to be desired to make one wise, she took of its fruit and ate; and she also gave some to her husband, who was with her, and he ate" (Gen 3:6 NRSV). Ultimately, the temptation of Adam and Eve led to sin when they ate the fruit that God had forbidden, and their sin introduced death into the world. Thus, Paul will write, "Just as sin came into the world through one man, and death came through sin, and so death spread to all because all have sinned" (Rom 5:13). From the very beginning, temptation has led through sin to death.

Fusing the Horizons

Many people in today's world use the word "temptation" lightly. After all, it's the brand name for a type of cat treat. And it's common to hear someone say, "Oh, that piece of cake looks so tempting." In a more serious

---

36. Moore-Keish 2019: 142.
37. McKnight 2011: 122.

mode, temptation may be seen as a struggle related to self-control. Some think that if one yields to temptation by indulging in whatever it is that has caught one's fancy, there's always another day when one can try again. In a post-Christian society James's connection of temptation to sin and death makes little sense. Non-religious western people understand "sin" as a religious word and might see it as related to violating God's rules. Yet for many westerners those rules are often seen as nonsensical. Instead, morality may consist of doing what is right for oneself and those around you and doing the least harm to others. The chain that James presents makes the most sense in a world that acknowledges God as Creator and Covenant Maker (we will look more carefully at the covenant/law in James when we study James 2) and understands humans as creatures in relationship with God. The status of this relationship does not need to be spelled out by James because he can rightly assume that those who read or heard his book would know and experience a covenant relationship with God. God made a covenant, a set of promises, to Israel and invited them to live in relationship with God in that covenant (Exod 19–24). When Jesus ate the last supper with the disciples, he indicated that he was offering and ratifying a new covenant in his blood (e.g., Luke 22:20). It is only within the reality of relationship with God that James's chain moving from temptation, to sin, to death makes sense. Ultimately, God is the giver of life and invites humanity into a living relationship with God. Since the beginning of the biblical narrative the consequence for sin, life lived apart from God, has been death. As people living in the twenty-first century, we must consider whether we still believe that God is the author of life and that God still invites his people to know and follow God's ways, ways that James will describe further in the sections that follow. If we affirm this belief in God as Creator and Covenant maker, then we will also affirm the work of resisting sinful temptation. Such resistance can take a variety of shapes in our time. For example, one can identify and acknowledge those places where one is most susceptible to temptation. The church can make acknowledgment of temptation normal and provide community, often in small groups, to encourage one another towards holiness of life. Similarly, the identification of sinful temptation may lead one to make concrete changes in one's life—no longer frequenting places or participating in activities that make it hard to resist temptation. And the identification of temptation may lead one to seek healing and renewal in one's inner life, perhaps in conversation with a spiritual director or Christian counselor, so that the inner fuel for temptation is reduced.

James

God's Good Gift, Life Itself (James 1:16–18)

The forceful instruction "do not be led astray" refers both backwards and forwards. Christians should be careful not to be misled in their understanding of God's nature. Looking backwards, they are not to think that God tempts human beings or is in anyway associated with evil. Looking forwards, they are to understand that God is clearly associated with goodness and is the giver of the very best gift, the gift of life.[38] Being deceived about the nature of who God is has the potential to draw the Christian into serious error, both in their understanding of God and in their understanding of the relationship between God and humanity. While James issues this strong warning, he also addresses them for the first time as his "beloved" family (here and Jas 1:19; 2:5). This term highlights the author's affection and care for the Christian kinship communities he addresses so strongly.

Having insisted that God does not tempt human beings, James now points to the origin of the good gifts that humans receive. He reiterates the idea twice. Each time, he emphasizes that he is talking about *every* gift. In Greek, the words used for "gift" are different, but they can be used interchangeably. It is possible that James repeats himself both for emphasis and for the pleasing rhythm the words form. The second portion reads "every *perfect* gift." James's opening saying ended with the idea that the person who endures testing becomes perfect—in other words, mature, whole, and without lack. Here, the use of "perfect" echoes that earlier saying and perhaps foreshadows the gift of the "perfect law" in Jas 1:25. Good and perfect gifts do not come from humanity but from above, from God. James has already described God as "the giving God" who gives openhandedly and without reproach (1:5). Now, we see that God's giving is rooted in his identity as Creator. Good and perfect gifts come down from the Father of lights. Although the Bible does not refer to God with the specific words "the Father of lights" anywhere else, this is clearly a reference to God as the creator of the heavenly lights: sun, moon, and stars. Creation itself is one of the many good gifts that God gives to his creatures along with the wisdom that James has already named (1:5). Unlike the creation that God has made, which is in a constant state of change and flux, God does not change.[39] James has already begun to build up a portrait of God. God is a giver (1:5) who is not tempted by evil, who doesn't tempt humans (1:13), and who

---

38. Moo 2000: 76.
39. Moo 2000: 79.

Commentary

is unchangeable. In other words, God's character is one that can be relied upon and trusted. In contrast to God, humans in James are people who experience trials and temptation (1:2–4; 12–15); are often subject to doubt or instability (1:6–8); can wither away like the flowers of the field (1:11); and are led astray by evil desires that lead from sin to death (1:14–15).

> *Gifts in the First Century (and Today):* In North America, we expect a gift to come without any expectations or obligations attached. In fact, if a gift is given with some kind of expectation or with strings attached, we often don't see it as a gift. Instead, something given with an expectation of a return may be an investment, a bribe, or an incentive based on the context. Our North American culture understands gifts as things that are willingly given by one party to another without an expectation of return.
>
> However, this understanding of gifts is quite foreign to the first century and to many contemporary cultures in our world today. In contrast to our contemporary western understanding of gifts, the cultures of the first century understood gift giving within a context of reciprocity. Those who gave gifts expected to receive something in return as well. In an important work on the topic of gift and how it relates to Paul, John Barclay writes:
>
>> When you are the recipient of the gift, it is crucial to give a well-measured return, if possible, with sufficient increment to place your friend under obligation (for when you need his aid). Such ordinary reciprocal favor excludes exact calculation but requires a rough awareness of who is under obligation to whom. Nonetheless, these are gifts—the exchange of services not a trade in goods—and it is crucial that they are suffused with the warm sentiments of "friendship."[40]
>
> When James talks about good and perfect gifts coming down from the Father of lights, first-century readers would not have seen these gifts as coming with "no strings attached." Instead, such good and perfect gifts would have created a relationship of obligation between the Creator and the creature who has received the good gifts. In James, one of the gifts that is received from God is the gift of life ("by his will he gave birth to us"). In the context of the first century, such a great gift indebted the recipient to the gift giver, God. One of the things that sets God apart from other first-century gift givers is that God gives his gifts indiscriminately. Within the first-century culture, many reserved their gifts for those they thought were worthy and who could reciprocate the generosity shown to

---

40. Barclay 2015: 25–26.

> them by responding with their own sets of gifts. But God does not reserve his gifts for those who can repay him but instead gives to all of humanity, even though they are unable to repay. Even those who receive the gift of the implanted word (see commentary on 1:18) are not able to fully reciprocate the gift they have been given. However, inability to reciprocate does not mean that the giver and the recipient are no longer in a relationship of obligation. The one who has received remains obligated to respond to the God who gives.
>
> While the western idea of gifts is one that rejects the idea that a gift comes with underlying obligations or expectations, the ethical requirements we place on those in public service shows that we understand that gifts may indeed carry expectations. We require politicians, judges, and others to disclose gifts they accept because we are aware that while in our own culture a gift may come without explicit expectations, it also has the potential to sway the decisions of those in power in favor of the gift giver. This reveals that while our own understanding of gifts has trended away from the first-century idea that gifts create obligation and reciprocity, we have not moved so far away as to be unaware of the potential for gifts to shape relationships and the use of power.

In Jas 1:14–15 evil desires give birth to sin and sin gives birth to death. Here, in Jas 1:18 we see that God also gives birth, but God brings forth "us" and God's birthing process produces life rather than death. Both of these births—the one that leads to sin and the one that leads to life are shaped by desire. But the two words used to describe God's desire and human desire are different in Greek. God's, *boulētheis*, is a verb meaning "wish, want, or desire"; while human desire, *epithumia*, is a noun meaning "desire, passion, lust." God's desire is pure. "'He willed,' emphasizes how God acted freely without external constraint in the creation of the universe and of humankind."[41] The unchanging God, who is the Father of lights and who gives good and perfect gifts, creates humanity and the whole cosmos because he wants to. God creates, gives birth, by the "word of truth." The language of birth may refer to the creation of the world, a creation that was initiated by God's voice. God spoke. It may also refer to the new birth that Christians experience through faith in Christ. The context of this verse draws on creation with such phrases as "Father of lights" and "creatures / what he created." But in the context of a book addressed to first-century

41. Martin 1988: 39.

Jewish Christians, the broader context of redemption cannot be completely ruled out, and the phrase "word of truth" is used in Paul to describe the good news (e.g., Eph 1:13; Col 1:5). In light of that, it is probable that the primary meaning may be drawn from the context of creation, but the allusion to salvation as new creation may already be well known in the Christian community. Robert Wall shows how the "word of truth" may refer to wisdom:

> Even as creation came by the "word of God" so also does the new creation come by agency of wisdom. Elsewhere in the New Testament, this same phrase refers to the gospel (Col 1:5–6). In the Old Testament, it refers to Torah (Ps 119:43), wisdom (cf. Prov 8:7, 30:5; Eccl 12:10; Sir 12:12) and the prophetic "word of the Lord" (cf. Isa 45:19). The common theological confession that stands behind these diverse biblical texts is that the actions of God are completely consistent with the word of God.[42]

The breadth of our understanding of the phrase "word of truth" will come into play as we consider such phrases as receiving "the implanted word" (v. 21) and being "doers of the word" (v. 22). The idea of the word as connected to the generative activity and wisdom of God impacts our understanding of the word Christians receive and practice. The result of birth by the "word of truth" is that those who are born in this way become "a kind of first fruits of his creatures." "First fruits" refers to the first produce to ripen at the beginning of a harvest. The first ripe apple or peach announces all the ripe fruit on the tree that will come in the weeks ahead. The term "first fruits" can refer both to priority in terms of order but also priority (e.g., status) in terms of kind. In other words, the creation of humanity may be seen as the pinnacle of God's creation, but the first fruits might also be set aside as a different kind, in other words the formation of the church community. Those who have been born out of God's desire and by the word of truth are now fashioned into a new community, a redemptive community that reveals God's ultimate purpose for all of creation: healing, restoration, and new creation. As the first fruits of God's creatures, this community becomes a sign of God's work and presence in the world. If the "word of truth" is understood to refer to creation, then humanity has a primary place in God's creation. Indeed, Genesis describes humankind as those to whom God has given the earth (Gen 1:28).[43] In this context, God's gift of life is contrasted with the

---

42. Wall 1997: 67.
43. Note that the language of subduing the earth and having dominion over it needs

child, Death, of earlier verses, and the imagery of "first fruits" draws out the kind of life the Creator provides, one of abundance and relationship and goodness. If the "word of truth" is understood as the means by which God gives life to those who have experienced God's redemption, then the image of "first fruits" may be one in which the redeemed stand as a sign of all those who have yet to be welcomed into the kingdom of God. They are the "first fruits" in the sense of being the first among many who will follow in the experience of redemption.

Fusing the Horizons

Western Protestants have long followed Paul in understanding salvation as a gift of God through faith in Jesus Christ. But James uses a different metaphor for salvation. It is a gift, but the gift that is given is the gift of new birth—new life. James's vision is rooted in the Creator and creation and invites Christians to understand themselves as part of God's fruitful created work. The language of gift creates an obligation on the part of the receiver to respond to the Creator who gives the gift of life. The new life that James envisions is one that is characterized by joy, endurance, wisdom, humility, and love. Such a life turns away from temptation and sin in order to turn towards the giving God who responds to trusting requests with generosity and open handedness. This is the life into which those born of the Father of lights enter.

---

to be understood in the ancient Near Eastern context in which it was written. In that context, a great king (here, God) gives responsibility for his land to a lesser king (here, humankind). The great king expects the lesser king to rule over the land as a steward. The language of dominion and rulership is one of stewardship rather than one of exploitation.

Receive the Word; Do the Word (James 1:19-25)

James 1:19-25: Take note of this, my beloved brothers and sisters: Everyone must be quick to hear, slow to speak, slow to anger; (20) for human anger does not produce the righteousness of God. (21) Therefore, put off all filth and the evil that is so prevalent and in humility receive the implanted word which is able to save you. And be doers of the word and not only hearers who deceive themselves. (23) Because if anyone is a hearer of the word and not a doer, this one is like a man who stares at his natural face in a mirror; (24) for he considers himself and having gone away immediately forgets what he was like. (25) But the one looking into the perfect law of freedom and abiding [in it] not being a forgetful hearer but a doer of work, this one will be blessed in what he does.

In Jas 1:19 our author seems to move abruptly to the topics of hearing, speaking, and anger. First, he reiterates the audience's position as beloved members of the community. James then writes a saying that would be equally at home in the book of Proverbs as it is in his letter. Richard Bauckham in his work on James has argued that James was a sage. A sage was a person who knew the wisdom of others and made it his own and then passed on that wisdom to others in his community. Bauckham argues that James knew the wisdom of the Old Testament, the popular wisdom literature of James's day (especially Ben Sira), and the wisdom of Jesus. He writes: "We can see James as a sage who has made the wisdom of Jesus his own. He does not repeat it; he is inspired by it. He creates his own wise sayings, sometimes as equivalents of specific sayings of Jesus, sometimes inspired by several sayings, sometimes encapsulating the theme of many sayings."[44] While working through the book of James, it will be clear that some sayings are particularly indebted to the sayings of Jesus. And some of Jesus's sayings also have roots in earlier Jewish traditions. In other words, Jesus himself was a sage who knew the traditions of his people.[45] This is not to say that Jesus was only a sage but rather that one important aspect of Jesus's life was his unique communication and embodiment of wisdom to those around him. The saying that James creates in 1:19 is his own way of expressing an idea that was common in both Old Testament and second temple wisdom literature. For example, "If you see a man hasty in speech, be sure there is more hope for a fool than for him" (Prov 29:20 NETS); "He who gives

---

44. Bauckham 1999: 82.
45. Witherington 1994.

an answer before listening—it is folly and reproach to him" (Prov 18:13 NETS); and, "A man who is slow to anger is better than the mighty, and he who controls his temper better than the one who captures a city" (Prov 16:32 NETS). Similarly, "Be quick in your hearing, and with long-suffering utter a reply. If you have understanding, answer your fellow, but if not, let your hand be upon your mouth" (Sir 5:11–12). James does not repeat any of these proverbs but rather creates his own proverbial saying that captures the theme of these sayings in a unique and memorable way. The quickness to listen is contrasted with slowness of speech and anger.

Scot McKnight writes: "Just what the members of the community are to listen *to* is not clear, though one thinks here that it might be to one another and to the 'other' in the community, to James's own counsel, to the gospel, to the Torah, to wisdom, or, what is contextually immediate, to the 'implanted word' of v. 21."[46] The first posture is listening. Only after that and only slowly come speech and anger. Note that neither of these things are forbidden; rather, they are limited. As Martha Moore-Keish reminds us even James himself expresses anger over the way the rich treat the poor (see Jas 5:1–6),[47] and the text does not say that one should never be angry. There are some things in this world that one must rightly speak against (such as the oppression of the poor by the wealthy) and times when it is right to be angry. However, in verse 20 a reason is given for being slow to anger. Notably human anger doesn't produce the same outcome that God's righteousness or justice would bring about. God's righteousness describes the way in which God sets the whole world to rights; in other words, it is only God who has the capacity to bring about perfect justice; it is only God who has the capacity to make all things right and well in the world. God's righteousness is not limited solely to his redemption of humanity but includes God's ability to make all things right. Human anger does not have the ability to produce that which can only come about from God's righteousness.

While the saying "quick to listen; slow to speak; slow to anger" begins a new section, the verses that follow still maintain connection with what came before.[48] Verses 14–15 show that people can be seduced by their de-

46. McKnight 2011: 137.
47. Moore-Keish 2019: 67.
48. This is perhaps a good place to remind ourselves that the most ancient manuscripts did not have paragraph breaks or even punctuation between sentences. While we break the text with punctuation for ease of reading and paragraphs for ease of understanding, these are later additions. Chapters (circa 1227 CE) and verses (circa 1555 CE) were added much later to aid the location of particular Scriptures.

sires and the outcome of that seduction is death for those who follow their desires. In contrast, verses 17–18 show that God's character is unchanging, and that God is the giver of all good gifts. It is God's will to give life to humans through God's word of truth. In light of the human tendency to sin and in light of God's creative work, the audience is to remove or put aside the filth of evil. This word "filth" will be used to describe the dirty and ragged clothes of the poor man in Jas 2:2, and it reminds the reader of the need to be clean. Similarly, evil can grow like a cancer or like weeds choking out the life of the Christians. Putting off filth and evil clears a space for the Christian to receive the implanted word, with humility. The word that they receive is one that is able to save. This implanted word describes further the word of truth by which God gives birth to humanity. As discussed above, the word of truth and the new birth it describes may be understood as a reference to creation, to new life available through God's redemption, or perhaps both.

> *Salvation and the Implanted Word*: Scholars debate the meaning of "the implanted word." In the early centuries of the church, many thought that the implanted word was natural law. For them, natural law was a set of unchanging moral principles authored by God and placed within humanity at creation. This was the means by which humans were able to know right and wrong.[49] Others have argued that the implanted word must refer to salvation since it is "the word that is able to save you." One possibility is that it refers to the salvation that is now available through the new covenant that is offered through Jesus Christ.[50] While Christians have the capacity to put off evil, they are also divinely empowered to act with virtue.[51] "The implanted word is not just the cause of the Christian life but also its ongoing power."[52] In a slightly different way, Boyce suggests that the implanted word refers to "the Word that is Jesus Christ in the incarnation."[53] If Jesus is the embodiment of wisdom, of the word of God, then Jesus and his wisdom are implanted within the new creature given birth by God.

49. Jackson-McCabe 2001.
50. Whitlark 2010.
51. Whitlark 2010: 152.
52. Whitlark 2010: 162.
53. Boyce 2015: 216.

Those who receive the implanted word do so with humility. Humility was not a Greco-Roman virtue, but it is highlighted as a posture within the early church. In Col 3:12 it is one of the elements Christians are instructed to put on. And in Titus 3:2, where the same word is translated "gentleness" in many English translations, it describes the attitude the leader is to have towards all people. James will use the word again to describe the behaviors that flow out of wisdom (3:13). Humility and gentleness are attributes of openness and vulnerability that create the environment to receive the implanted word.

Fusing the Horizons

The call to listen while being slow to speak and slow to anger is just as relevant now as it has been for two thousand years. In a world of political polarization that has entered into the church, the need for care in listening, for self-control, and restraint in emotion are more necessary than ever. Indeed, speaking too quickly and allowing anger to run its course can destroy Christian fellowship in myriad ways. There are multiple practices that the church teaches to encourage Christians to put off all forms of evil and sin. Among these are confession—both corporate confession in worship and private confession to another person of faith such as a pastor, priest, spiritual director, or a trusted fellow Christian. Alongside of practices such as confession, accountability, and seeking restoration of relationships is the instruction to receive the implanted word. Part of the transformation of Christians takes place when they are open and vulnerable and able to hear and receive the true word that God wishes to speak into their lives. In contrast to the words of this world that tear down and destroy, which may be driven by fear, unrighteous anger, jealousy, self-promotion, and other evils, God's word of truth is deeply creative and generative, producing life in the Christian. God's word is not limited to one truth or one message or one reality. Instead, it embodies the wisdom of God demonstrated in the person of Jesus with love, truth, and kindness. How does the Christian hear and receive the true word of God? This is part of listening, a posture that recognizes that he or she is not enough, and that there is always more to learn and experience from God. Such a posture encourages ears that are eager to listen—to Jesus the Word, to the biblical text, to the Holy Spirit, to Christian teachers. Such a posture trusts that God's word is stronger, wiser, and deeper than any word by which the world might want to limit or define the person who has experienced the birth that comes from the Creator.

Those Who Do the Word Receive Blessing (James 1:22-25)

How does one receive a word? One receives by hearing, by listening. The word that is implanted is a word that has been deeply heard, a word that is received from the Creator and that harkens back first to creation itself and then to the word of Jesus—both his message and Jesus himself. For James, it is not enough to receive that word via hearing; the person who hears the word well will also be a person who acts based on that received word. Those who think that it is sufficient simply to hear the word without corresponding action are deluding themselves about the very nature of the word they have heard. To think that the word does not require action is to be deceived. And the one doing the deceiving is the very person who thinks that action is not required. In other words, this is another temptation that the Christian in James faces—the temptation to think that hearing and receiving alone are sufficient for Christian faith. In Jas 1:22, James states this instruction positively: be doers of the word. In the next verse, the instruction is stated negatively: "If anyone is not a doer of the word, he is like . . ."

James tells a short parable to illustrate the principle that one must both hear and act upon the implanted word. In this parable a man contemplates his face in a mirror. In other words, he looks at himself in a mirror and thinks about the way he has turned out and what he really looks like.[54] He studied himself, and then he goes away from the mirror. James stresses that immediately the man forgets what sort of person he was like. There is an absurdity to this parable. How can a person who has carefully studied himself immediately forget what kind of person he is? That very absurdity is part of James's point. How can the person who has experienced the saving reality of the implanted word forget what sort of person that implanted word creates? The one who has received the implanted word should expect that such a word produces something in the life of the one who received it. The outcome of the received word is action appropriate to the word itself.

Right action, however, does not come from gazing at oneself in the mirror but rather from looking into the perfect law (1:25). This is the first mention of the law in James. The opening section of James 2 will discuss the

---

54. BDAG, 192, defines the Greek phrase *prosopon tēs geneseōs autou* as "his natural face" and explains that phrase as above.

law more fully, and the law is also an important part of the saying in Jas 4:11. There are various debates among scholars about what James is referring to when he mentions the law. James as a good Jew would have known the law, the Torah, well. In addition, he is writing to Jewish Christians who would also know and love the law. In that setting, it makes perfect sense to understand "the law" as the Torah, the instructions that God gave to Israel in the Pentateuch as part of his covenant relationship with them. Other scholars have argued that "the law" refers to the good news about Jesus, particularly as it is understood through the implanted word (e.g., Ralph Martin, who explicitly says that "the word" and "the law" are the same). But these two understandings of the law do not need to be separated from each other in a hard and fast manner. For early Jewish Christians the law remained the means of staying in relationship with God, and they came to see Jesus as the fulfillment of that law. Thus Jesus says, "Do not think that I have come to abolish the law or the prophets; I have come not to abolish but to fulfill" (Matt 5:17). The law is perfected, fulfilled, and brought to maturity in Jesus. It is important to note that the law is not simply a list of rules or a set of regulations. Instead, the Torah contains all kinds of instruction designed to help Israel understand its history as the people whom God delivered from slavery, and with whom God covenanted both at Sinai and in the land of Israel. The Torah is a record of that covenant history and of the promises, commands, wisdom, and instructions that relate to that covenant.

As westerners we often think about freedom in the sense of being unencumbered or having no responsibilities. In other words, law and freedom in our western understanding are often opposites. But here, the law is explicitly associated with freedom. In other words, freedom is found not through the removal of responsibility but rather through being embedded in good communal relationships with God and with others. Indeed, when James defines the law further, he will point to the action of loving one's neighbor as oneself as the definition of the law (2:8). But how does this law bring freedom? Instead of worrying about oneself and whether one is free, the person who looks into the perfect law sees God, sees his neighbor, and sees the self clearly; the very act of seeing the neighbor in right relationship with the self frees the person who looks into the law from self-absorption. The person who looks into the law of freedom is ultimately freed from evil and instead bound with love, which brings about flourishing both for the individual and the community. This understanding of the nature of the law is tied up with James's identification of the law with the practice of loving one's neighbor. Unlike the person who looked at himself in the mirror and went away, the person who looks into the law also remains in the law. In other words, the action of loving God and loving neighbor characterizes the ongoing life of the one who follows God's law and meditates and reflects and abides in that law. Once again, James reiterates that this person is not a forgetful hearer. This is not the person who looked in the mirror, went away, and forgot what kind of person he was. The person whose life is oriented around loving one's neighbor doesn't forget the word that shapes this kind of life. Instead, this is a life characterized by being a doer of work. Scot McKnight comments on what "work" refers to in this context:

> The "work" of 1:25b is most likely, then, compassion (deeds of mercy) and holiness, and it needs to be seen in the context of a letter written to the poor and for the poor. James is here expressing the need for solidarity among the poor and care for one another. The substance of his letter emerges as we read this in context: those who follow Jesus' interpretation of the Torah (1:25a) care for the poor, as he did, and know that God's plan is to establish justice, as is seen in the Magnificat (Luke 1:46–55). Such people do not lash out in violence (1:13–15, 19–20) but pursue God's justice in humility (1:21) and peacefulness (3:18). To speak of "persevering in the Law" is ... a summons for the messianic community to stick together as the first fruits (1:18), to remain faithful to Jesus and the Jesus Creed, to avoid succumbing to the pressures of the rich (1:12), and to pursue God's justice in peace and humility (1:21; 3:18).[55]

The one who is a doer and not a forgetful hearer receives a promise: this one will be blessed in his doing. For the second time, James uses a beatitude to point to the honor that God will give to the one who lives out the law of love, the perfect law, the law of freedom in their daily actions towards others. That honor is still future but is guaranteed with God's promise.

Fusing the Horizons

Most Protestants who have been around the church for any length of time have heard and embraced the doctrine that salvation is by faith alone. Perhaps one of the most famous verses related to this doctrine is Eph 2:8–9: "For by grace you have been saved through faith; and this is not your own

---

55. McKnight 2011: 161–62.

doing; it is the gift of God—not the result of works, so that no one may boast." Often Protestants stop at these two verse and fail to read on to the next verse, which continues, "For we are what he has made us, created in Christ Jesus for good works which God prepared beforehand to be our way of life" (Eph 2:10). As Protestants, the focus has often been on the first two verses and on an understanding that salvation is a free, undeserved gift from God and that the only response that is needed is trust in God. However, sometimes this focus on the gift of salvation has detracted from the final verse (Eph 2:10) with its emphasis on doing good works. In contrast, James focuses heavily on doing and not only on being or receiving. In James, salvation is received through the gift of the implanted word and is evidenced in the life of faithful action. James's understanding of salvation is deeply rooted in creation, in God's word implanted into the believer, and in the believer's openness to receiving that word. This is a reminder that our salvation comes from the Creator. And the Creator who implants his creative word invites creative action, "work," in response. James will expand our understanding of both the type of speech and the kind of action, "works," that are part of the Christian life in the chapters to come.

True Religion (James 1:26-27)

James 1:26-27: If anyone considers himself to be religious and does not bridle his tongue but deceives his heart, the religion of that one is vain. (27) Pure and undefiled religion in the presence of God the father is this: to visit orphans and widows in their distress, to keep oneself unstained by the world.

In the first-century world, being an honorable person was one of the greatest cultural values of the time. One of the ways that both Jews and Romans demonstrated their honorable nature was through their religious practices. For Romans this included proper worship and respect for the gods. For Jews this included offering sacrifices at the temple in Jerusalem when they were able and following ritual practices such as circumcision, Sabbath rest, and food laws. James does not point to any of these things as the marker of a religious person. First, James indicates that people who consider themselves to be religious but who can't control their speech are deceiving themselves about the value of their religious practice. This is reminiscent of Jesus's saying that what comes out of a person reveals the true inner workings of the person (Matt 15:18; Luke 6:45). Throughout James, speech is a key indicator of the character of a person and their relationship to God. Already we have been pointed to the person who asks for wisdom with trust that God will give it (1:5-6) and we have seen the instruction to be slow to speak (1:19). In the chapters ahead we will come across the rejection of speech that shows favoritism (2:1-4), an essay on the tongue (3:1-12), and implications of lying, deceit, and boasting (3:13-18). Appearing outwardly religious without having control of one's speech undermines any claim to religious wisdom or knowledge. Indeed, to claim to be religious without controlling one's speech is to lie to oneself about one's religious status.

More positively, James identifies two components of the religious life. The first is to visit widows and orphans in their distress. Throughout the Old Testament the widow and the orphan are identified as the most vulnerable members of Jewish society. These are the ones to whom God's care is especially extended. The Psalmist describes God as "Father of orphans and protector of widows" (Ps 68:3). And these are the ones that God calls Israel to care for with special consideration. They are not to "remove an ancient landmark or encroach on the fields of orphans" (Prov 23:10). And they are reminded that those who seem vulnerable have a strong redeemer

James

who will plead their case (Prov 23:11). When the prophets accuse Israel of going astray from their covenant relationship with God, they accuse Israel of preying on widows and orphans (Isa 10:2; Jer 5:28; Ezek 22:7). In the agrarian world of both the Old and New Testaments, widows and orphans faced particular vulnerabilities. Without a male head of household to help provide for the family, widows could find themselves struggling to work and maintain property, to pay debts, and to provide for any children. Both orphans and widows were vulnerable to having their land and other resources appropriated by unscrupulous or greedy relatives. God despised such treatment of the vulnerable in the Old Testament. James instructs his readers to visit widows and orphans. The word "visit" (*episkeptesthai*) has several possible meanings, including: "1. To make a careful inspection, look at, examine; 2. To go to see a person with helpful intent, visit; 3. To exercise oversight in behalf of, look after, make an appearance to help."[56] When James instructs his readers to visit widows and orphans, he is instructing them to do what is necessary in order to support, care for, look after, and help them. Indeed, in the early church it would become the role of bishops (*episkopos*, overseer) to make sure that widows and orphans received the help that they needed.[57]

The second instruction is to keep oneself unstained by the world. This is the first use of "the world" in James. In the context of James, "the world" stands for the moral system that is in opposition to God (cf. Jas 4:4). The book of James, like other wisdom literature, presents readers with two choices, one of which is in alignment with God and the other which is alienated from God. Already in chapter 1, we have seen trust versus doubt (1:6); being driven by our own desire towards sin or receiving God's desire for us, the implanted word (1:14–18); and putting off evil and receiving that which can save (1:21). Now, readers are instructed to pursue purity. "Purity is a boundary marker indicating the point of no return between James's audience and wider Greco-Roman culture.... Understanding purity in James as separation from the world is evidence not of a call to sectarian rejection of all social-cultural contact, but of a nuanced stance toward Greco-Roman culture."[58] Such a stance takes seriously the call to purity as a framework for wholeness and integrity in relationship with God and one another while rejecting the values of the world. Together these two instructions form

---

56. BDAG, 378.
57. Allison 2013: 362.
58. Lockett 2008: 188.

a summary of the first chapter of James and set the direction for major themes on purity and care for the vulnerable in the chapters ahead.

Fusing the Horizons

When students study the book of James with me, one of the questions that often surfaces is whether the instruction to visit widows and orphans still applies to our contemporary society. In western culture, where we are highly independent rather than interdependent, it can be tempting to think that the government will take care of the needs of widows, orphans, and other vulnerable people. However, both the Old and New Testament demonstrate that God places a high value on care for the vulnerable. In fact, when the church cares for the poor and vulnerable among them they become witnesses to the world around them. In the ancient world, it was considered unwise to give to those who could not repay. And care for the destitute was seen as a waste of time, energy, and money.[59] In contrast, both Jews and then Christians understood that God had a special concern for the poor and vulnerable and worked to provide for their needs. Those who are vulnerable both within our churches and outside of them continue to need the special care of God's people. One simple way that this has been practiced is by gathering teams of men within the church to adopt a widow, a single-mom, or another person in need and to serve them on a monthly basis so that they know that they are cared for. Those who have participated in such ministries find that they are more deeply in love with God, more committed to God's people, and more ready to testify about what God has been doing among them.[60] The instruction to visit and care for the vulnerable remains one of the defining instructions of the church.

For some who come from particular strands of conservative religious tradition, "keeping oneself unstained by the world" has meant avoiding "worldly" activities like dancing and movies and "worldly ways" like wearing jewelry and makeup. But these things are about outward appearances just like offering sacrifices in the temple or keeping Sabbath were outward religious practices for Jews in the first century. Of course, these things can be undertaken in the right spirit and can even be a means for deepening relationship with God and others. But these things *in themselves* are not

---

59. Barclay 2020: 27.

60. For one example, see https://newcommandment.lpages.co/how-meeting-to-meet-needs-ministers.

the source of purity. Instead, striving for purity in relationship with God will involve not only outward works, such as rightly oriented speech and care for the poor and vulnerable, but also inward characteristics, such as wisdom, peace, gentleness, genuineness, and nonjudgmental attitudes towards others.

Commentary

Love Your Neighbor (James 2:1–13)

James 2:1–13: My brothers and sisters, do not hold the faith of our glorious Lord Jesus Christ with acts of favoritism. (2) For if a man with a gold ring enters into a synagogue wearing fine clothing, and also a poor man enters wearing filthy clothing, (3) and you look with favor on the one wearing the bright clothing and you say, "you sit here in a good place," and to the poor one you say, "you stand or sit there by my footstool," (4) then have you not discriminated among yourselves and become judges with evil reasoning? (5) Listen, my beloved brothers and sisters, has not God chosen those who are poor in the eyes of the world to be rich in faith and heirs of the kingdom which he promised to those who love him? (6) But you dishonor the poor. Do not the rich lord it over you and are not these the ones who drag you into court? (7) Do not these blaspheme the good name which is called over you?

(8) If on the one hand you fulfill the royal law according to the scripture, "Love your neighbor as yourself," you do well. (9) If on the other hand you show partiality, you commit sin being convicted by the law as trespassers. (10) For whoever keeps the whole law, but stumbles in one part, has become liable of all. (11) For the one who said, "Do not commit adultery," also said, "Do not murder." But if you do not commit adultery, but you murder, you have become a transgressor of the law.

(12) In this manner speak and in this manner act as those about to be judged through the law of freedom. (13) For judgment [is] without mercy to the one not doing mercy; mercy triumphs over judgment.

Chapter 1 introduced the major themes of James: wisdom, speech, care for the poor, the law, faith, and works. The remainder of the book mainly consists of longer sections of text that expand on these themes—a sort of collection of mini essays. James shows his kinship with his readers when he begins this section with the address, my brothers and sisters. He then begins a new section of the letter that condemns giving preference to the rich over the poor. The section begins with a short story about a rich man and a poor man who both enter a synagogue but are treated very differently (2:1–4). In verses 5–7 he asserts that God has chosen the poor over the rich who abuse them. Next, verses 8–11 provide a basis for acting without favoritism: the law of loving one's neighbor. Finally, in verses 12–13 the section wraps up with a reminder that they should speak and act as people who will be judged by the law. Here James draws out the relationship between judgment and mercy. It is quite possible that "James 2:1–13 and 5:1–6 frame the entire [body of the] letter with the indictment of the wealthy. It is clear from this *inclusion* that 'the wealthy' are the main antagonists in the letter and are the recipients of James's harshest critiques."[61] At the same time, all those who hear and respond well to James will embrace an ethic of love toward their neighbor.

An Example of Favoritism (James 2:1–4)

James 2:1 opens with a strong proclamation that there are two things that cannot be held together. One can either have faith in the risen Lord Jesus Christ or one can show unfair bias towards some people over others. Faith in Jesus is incompatible with displays of prejudice towards others. This is the second and last time that James explicitly names Jesus Christ in this book. Here, he is identified as "Lord," indicating his position of power, authority, and rulership. As Lord, Jesus is one to be honored and obeyed. When the Old Testament was translated from Hebrew to Greek, the Jewish translators chose the Greek word *kurios*, "Lord," for God's name. When James refers to Jesus as Lord, he points to Jesus's shared identity with God, including sharing in God's authority, power, and glory. God's glory refers to his pure, shining character and to the weight of it which fills the temple and spreads out from there into the land God gave to the Jews and to the world beyond. Jesus Christ is identified as the glorious Lord or the Lord of Glory, as one who reveals the radiant transcendence of God. This radiance is now contained in the human person of Jesus in his incarnation when Jesus humbled himself to take on a human body. And this glory is revealed in the resurrection body of Jesus that now shares in God's glory. As the Christ, a word that means "anointed" and refers to Jesus's kingship in the line of David, Jesus, the truly glorious Lord shares in the reign of God. It is this person, the glorious Lord Jesus Christ, whom James's audience trusts. The man who associated with the poor, the vulnerable, and the despised without losing his authority as glorious Lord and King cannot be associated with prejudice or favoritism or partiality by those who claim to follow him.

James follows up his declaration that prejudice or favoritism is incompatible with trust in Jesus with an illustration (vv. 2–3). Two very different people come into the synagogue. In the first century, synagogues served a variety of purposes. They were places of study, prayer, and communal

---

61. Coker 2015: 111.

gathering. "The synagogue also served as a law court for community matters, with authority to mete out punishments such as the thirty-nine lashes suffered repeatedly by Paul (2 Cor 11:24; cf. Matt 10:17; Acts 22:19; *m. Mak.* 3:10–11)."[62] James 2:1–13 repeatedly refers to "judges, judging, courts, and the law," which leads many to see the setting here as one in which a rich person and a poor person enter the synagogue in the context of a dispute or a court case, and where the rich one is shown favor over the poor one.[63] Such favoritism is expressly forbidden in the Old Testament. For example, Lev 19:15 says, "You shall not render an unjust judgment; you shall not be partial to the poor or defer to the great; with justice you shall judge your neighbor." Others see the setting here as one in which the assembly has gathered for worship.[64] Showing favoritism has no place in worship just as it has no place in court, but the setting here is more likely a dispute being brought for settlement. The illustration continues: A man wearing a gold ring and dressed in fine clothing enters. The other man is poor and wearing filthy clothes. The rich man is shown to a good seat. The poor man is told to "stand or sit here by my footstool." This quick sketch draws on the cultural values and assumptions of the ancient world. One of the most important values of the ancient world was the ascription of honor to people in society. To be given a good seat is to be honored. To be given a low seat ("the footstool") is to be dishonored. Here, preferential treatment is given to the man with good clothes and a gold ring while the poor man is treated with contempt. The favoritism that is shown to one man over the other is a form of judgment. Those who are looking at the two people have drawn a set of conclusions about who is worthy to sit where.

Clothes are an important means of declaring one's status. A person who came into the synagogue wearing fine clothing and a gold ring was declaring their status not just as a person of means but as a person who belongs to a particular social status within a very hierarchical society. Jason Coker notes that "the equestrian order was wealthy, wore distinctive dress, and their primary income came from landownership. All three of these characteristics are specifically condemned in 2:1–13 and 5:1–6. Garments and accessories were not simply for decoration; they were specifically symbolic of one's rank in Roman society. Only Roman citizens could wear togas

---

62. Wagner 2000: 800.
63. Allison 2013: 370–72.
64. Adamson 1976: 105.

and tunics, whereas gold rings specifically marked the equestrian order."[65] In contrast, the poor man is described as wearing dirty, shabby clothes. These clothes mark the man as undeserving of respect and attention. James's description of the two men portrays the vast gulf between the rich man and the poor man, the way in which each one was treated differently, and how honor was shown to one over the other.

In verse 4, the illustration began with an "if" and ends with this question: "Then have you not discriminated among yourselves and become judges with evil reasoning?" The question expects the answer, "Yes, you have." In a final twist to the illustration, the reader sees that not only have the rich man and the poor man been judged but the gathered assembly is also judged. If those who are gathered show favoritism, then they can be identified as judges whose rulings are created from evil thinking. In both Jewish and Greco-Roman court systems, impartiality was a strong value (even if not perfectly upheld) and violating the ideal of impartiality could reveal the status of the judge as less than honorable.

God Chooses the Poor (James 2:5–7)

In contrast to their choice of the rich over the poor, James reminds his beloved brothers and sisters that God chose the poor in the world to be rich in faith and heirs to the kingdom (v. 5). The verse begins with a reiteration of their family connection—"brothers and sisters"—that draws out the kinship of those who hear this instruction. And James adds to this address the word "beloved," showing his affection for those he writes to. This is God's new family made up of those who belong to the glorious risen Lord, Jesus Christ. James catches their attention with the instruction "listen," and tells them what God has to say about the poor. God chooses the poor. This saying of James is reminiscent of Jesus's words recorded in Luke 6:20, "Blessed are you who are poor, for yours is the kingdom of God." In both the Old and New Testaments, we see that God has a particular concern for the poor. In the Old Testament, God instructs that the rich were to leave parts of their harvest for the poor (Lev 19:9–10), were to take poor relatives into their homes as needed (Lev 25:35–36), and were not to show favoritism towards either the rich or the poor in court (Lev 19:15). In the New Testament, Luke's Gospel shows a special concern for the poor from the very beginning. In Mary's song she sings about a God who "has filled the hungry with

---

65. Coker 2015: 123.

good things, and sent the rich away empty" (Luke 1:53). And when Jesus begins his ministry, his declaration starts by proclaiming a message drawn from Isaiah 61 in which he announces that God's Spirit is upon him to declare good news to the poor (Luke 4:18). At the great feast (Luke 14:13), the invitation is extended to the poor. And in Luke's gospel we meet the poor widow who gives everything she has and is commended by Jesus (Luke 21:1–4). This is just one example from one book of the New Testament of God's concern for the poor. In western contexts, God's choosing of the poor can seem unfair. I suspect that this derives from a western focus that people should be chosen based on their skill or ability (i.e., meritocracy). Elsa Tamez's work on James comes from a Latin American perspective. She indicates early in her book that "a Latin American reading of the epistle... fixes its gaze on the oppressed.... From the angle of oppression from which we are reading James, we must adopt the perspective of the oppressed, which, we believe, is that of James."[66] As westerners, we often read from the perspective of "the rich," asking questions about why they are judged so harshly or unfairly or without hope of repentance, but reading from the perspective of the poor shows that God's choice of the poor provides hope to those whose lives might lead to despair and hopelessness. In her next chapter, Tamez provides significant insight on the poor in James 2 and is worth quoting at length:

> James refers here to the poor in both a concrete way and in a general sense, not only to those who get no seat in church and are treated badly.
>
> It is worth recalling the uniqueness of God's preference for the poor. This was unheard of and scandalous for other religions. In the Greek world, for example, there is no other god who has this preferential inclination for the poor.
>
> ... What does it mean to be rich in faith? I think that it must have a very important meaning for the poor. To be rich in faith cannot be relegated solely to a spiritual plane, completely disconnected from their situation of poverty and suffering. To be rich in faith includes more than being open to the Spirit with more naturalness than the rich. It does indeed include being more sensitive to the presence of God, but it includes something more: *it means to hope in the promise of God's reign.* This is the reign inaugurated by Jesus as he cured the sick, restored dignity to the outcast, raised the dead. So to be rich in faith must be understood in the same

---

66. Tamez 2002: 21.

way as to be heirs of God's reign. Reading this text from the angle of hope we can imagine how much the words must have meant for the oppressed.[67]

What is hard to wrap our heads around is that God can at one and the same time choose one group, showing them special attention, without excluding another group. God's special care and attention towards the poor and marginalized does not have to exclude people who do not belong to the margins; although, notice that "the rich" in James are repeatedly described as people engaged in oppression, lawsuits, stealing, and abuse—people who in their current state are not welcome in God's kingdom. For these, the only right action is the repentance described in Jas 4:7–10. God does indeed choose the poor over the wealthy who use their resources to abuse others for their own self advancement.

The Old Testament describes a particular group of poor known as the *anawim* who are shown favor because they remain faithful to God amid their difficult circumstances. For this group, poverty and piety are closely related.[68] While James does describe the poor as "those who love him" (2:5), there is not a special focus on piety, and readers should be careful not to lessen the significance of God's choosing by asserting that somehow poverty and piety are always connected. Again, Elsa Tamez rejects readings of James that see the poor as devout people without any concerns about prosperity instead asserting, "The hungry, the exploited, the jobless want at least to satisfy their basic necessities, and they turn to God with those hopes."[69]

In James, those who are part of the assembly disrespect the poor person who enters the synagogue. In this way, their values are more in line with the values of the world than the values of God.[70] The world is made up of all that which is counter to God's values and God's ways. In the eyes of the world, those without material resources are despised, unworthy of the attention of those with resources, but in God's eyes the poor are chosen. They are specifically chosen to be rich in faith and heirs of God's kingdom. Those with little find themselves to be dependent upon God and thus leaning into God with trust for their very survival. These are the ones who will inherit the kingdom. God's reign is evident from Creation onwards in Scripture. In various Old Testament texts God is described as sitting on a throne or

67. Tamez 2002: 37 (emphasis added).
68. McKnight 2011: 195.
69. Tamez 2002: 37.
70. Johnson 1995: 224.

as being enthroned on the cherubim (1 Sam 4:4; 2 Kgs 9:15; Ps 9:7–11; Isa 6:1). The rule of God is envisioned as one in which the ruler "judges the world with righteousness" and serves as "a stronghold for the oppressed, a stronghold in times of trouble" (Ps 9:8–9). In the New Testament, Jesus comes proclaiming the kingdom of God, an upside-down kingdom in which the poor are promised the kingdom of heaven, the needs of the hungry and thirsty are met, and the meek inherit the earth (Matt 5:3–11; Luke 6:20–26). This kingdom is proclaimed by Jesus, inaugurated by his death on a cross, and exists now as the rule of the risen Son enthroned alongside his Father until the time the Son returns. This is the kingdom that the poor of James inherit. By designating the poor as heirs of the kingdom, James elevates the poor from a marginalized group to a position of honor within the community. The riches of the poor are not located in their possessions but rather in their trust in God's reign and God's care and provision. Thus, they are rich in faith. This kingdom has been promised to those who love God. A promise is a speech-act in which someone indicates that in the future they will make reality match the word that is spoken now. A promise is only as reliable as the person who makes the promise. No promise maker is more reliable than God. Here, James reminds his audience that God's promise of the kingdom is made to the very people who have experienced discrimination within the religious and social systems of their day. This marginalized group is now identified as rich in faith, indeed as those who love God. It is possible that the promise starts with the poor who love God and that from there the promise extends to encompass all who love God. But in the midst of an argument against unjust favoritism, it is clear that the poor are those to be imitated for their faith and that any claim to loving God cannot include discrimination.

Rich, poor, and in-between: economic life in the first century: Sometimes it is hard for us to imagine how different life was two thousand years ago. You might start by closing your eyes and eliminating everything you can think of that runs on electricity or a motor. Whole areas of our modern life are eliminated (the transportation industry; electronics, computing, and the world wide web; heating and cooling; construction equipment; the modern grocery store; and the list goes on). Instead, the ancient world depended on physical labor, local markets, and basic travel at a maximum speed of three or four miles an hour.

In this world, most people worked as part of an agricultural economy and lived at subsistence level. This meant that a great deal of the population was one farming season away from disaster. Others, who were considered poor, lived below this subsistence level: these were often day laborers, people who were disabled or sick, or people who had no family to care for them in their old age. Such people were truly destitute. There were no safety nets provided by the government, and family networks were an important means of survival for those with limited resources. Even though this was an agricultural economy, there were many different types of work that families might engage in. In addition to basic farming and husbandry there were many other types of work, especially in the cities. These included such things as butchers, bakers, launderers, traders, merchants, storekeepers, construction workers, bankers, secretaries, and others. There was always the possibility that someone could excel and rise up above the subsistence level. At the same time, life was precarious for many in the first century.

Only 2–3 percent of the population were rich and perhaps only another 15–20 percent of the population lived above the subsistence level.[71] The rich were usually those with power: Caesar and his family, Roman senators and equestrians, provincial governors, high priests, and those who assisted this group had resources. Often these resources could be used to add even more wealth to their balance sheets (see Jas 5:1–6). The temptation on the part of the wealthy to abuse their power for financial profit was ubiquitous. Among those who were rich, manual labor was considered degrading: an activity fit only for those of lower status. The one exception to this was the "gentleman farmer" who "worked" an estate with the assistance of an overseer and slaves. The rich acted as benefactors to cities, often demonstrating their generosity and appreciation for a place through the giving of gifts ("benefits"). "Benefactors financed civic life, paying for entertainments, festivals, public buildings (e.g., temples, theaters, baths, gymnasia, stoas, markets) and public-works projects (e.g., city walls, aqueducts, fountains, sewers, roads, harbors)."[72]

---

71. Identifying the percentage of people at various levels of the economic scale is challenging and scholars have debated the exact percentages of people at various levels. Some evidence points to the first century as a more prosperous time than some other centuries. However, even at the most generous reading, scholars estimate the percentages for the wealthy elite at 2 to 3 percent and those with moderate surplus at 22 to 30 percent. Longenecker 2009: 245.

72. Walker 2000: 158.

Commentary

> The economic foundation of the Roman Empire was a system of patronage in which wealthy patrons provided for lower status clients. Those who accepted "gifts" from a patron entered a long-term relationship of debt and obligation:
>
>> In a world in which wealth and property were concentrated into the hands of a very small percentage of the population, the majority of people often found themselves in need of assistance in one form or another and therefore had to seek the patronage of someone who was better placed in the world. . . . Patrons might be asked to provide money, grain, employment or land. . . . One who received such a benefit became a client to the patron, accepting the obligation to publicize the favor and his or her gratitude for it, thus contributing to the patron's reputation.[73]
>
> The lives of the rich and the poor were intertwined, but in a world that was built on both patronage and honor, honor often accrued to the wealthy at the expense of the poor. It was the rich who could be praised as generous, good, and kind, while it was the poor who exalted the rich with their loyalty, service, and praise.
>
> We might note here at the end of this exploration of the roles of the rich and the poor that James does not seem to see most of his audience as belonging to either of these categories. On the one hand, they are clearly not the rich. The rich are never addressed or explicitly identified as "brothers and sisters" who belong to the community that James writes to. On the other hand, they are instructed to care for the poor: for widows, orphans, and people who come begging at their doors. This implies that they have enough to share with others and are thus not part of the truly destitute.[74]

In 2:6–7 James draws a sharp contrast between the poor who love God and have been chosen by him and the activities of the rich. The rich oppress, dominate, and exploit those in James's audience. They drag people into court using the courts as part of their way of harassing God's people. And they make false and damaging statements about the name of Jesus, the very name that identifies those to whom James writes. In the illustration that begins this chapter, we see that James already identifies the inclination of the audience to prefer the rich over the poor. Now we find out that not only is outward appearance no sure judge of character, but that the lives of the rich might be summed up by words such as arrogant, blasphemous, greedy, and

73. DeSilva 2000: 767.
74. Bauckham 1999: 188.

harsh. They use their power to dominate the poor. The LXX translation of Amos uses this same Greek word to describe the sin of oppressing the poor when he writes, "Hear this, you that trample on the needy, and bring to ruin the poor of the land, saying, . . . 'We will make the ephah small and the shekel great, and practice deceit with false balances, buying the poor for silver and the needy for a pair of sandals" (Amos 8:4–6). These are the actions of people with power who use that power to accumulate more and more at the expense of those who are unable to defend themselves from the abuse of power. These same people are described as people who use the courts not for justice but for greedy gain. While the expectation in both Greco-Roman and Jewish culture was that justice would be distributed without favoritism, the reality was often far different. It is the rich person, the one associated with these kinds of abuses, who is shown deference in the illustration that begins our chapter. Showing preference for the rich person is to put one's weight behind the values of society, which honors those with resources often regardless of their character. Meanwhile, to align oneself with the poor is to align oneself with a group of people for whom God has shown special regard. Having established that the favoritism shown to a rich person entering the synagogue is misaligned with God's values (2:1–7), James can now clearly articulate the choice before them. In the two ways theology that is evident throughout James, the choice is laid out as either fulfilling the royal law summed up in the instruction "love your neighbor as yourself (2:8)," or sinning by giving preferential treatment to the wealthy (2:9).

The Law of Love (James 2:8-13)

James 2:8 is the second time that James mentions the law. Previously, he described a person who looks into "the perfect law of liberty" and acts upon it as blessed in what he does (1:25). Now, in verses 8–12 James returns to and expands on the theme of "the law." Scholars suggest three possible ways to think about the law in Jas 2:8. First, the law refers to the Torah, the first five books of the Old Testament.[75] Other parts of the New Testament use the word law in this manner. For example, Jesus says, "Do not think that I have come to abolish the law and the prophets; I have come not to abolish but to fulfill" (Matt 5:17). Here, Jesus uses the word "law" to speak of the Pentateuch in his declaration that he is not abolishing but fulfilling the law. James's letter to a Jewish audience also supports the understanding that the

---

75. Dibelius 1975: 142.

word "law" refers to the Torah. Second, another group argues that the word "law" here refers specifically to the instruction to "love your neighbor as yourself" quoted from Lev 19:18.[76] Both in the immediate context of the settling of a dispute and in the wider context of a book that focuses on living faithfully in relationship to God, James emphasizes the law of loving one's neighbor. Finally, another group understands "the law" here as a reference to the Torah now brought to its fulfillment in Jesus and thus as a reference to the good news.[77] This group of scholars notes that Jesus sums up all the law and the prophets in two commandments: the commandment to love the Lord your God with all your heart, soul, and mind, and the commandment to love your neighbor as yourself (Matt 22:37–40). Allison seems right to note that here the law of love is a part standing for the whole law.[78] And it is also appropriate to assume that the early Christian community would have been aware of Jesus's appropriation of this commandment as one of the two great commandments. In Luke's Gospel, Jesus answers the question, "Who is my neighbor?" with the story of the Good Samaritan. There, the Samaritan is lifted up as the one who shows mercy to the vulnerable man in need at the side of the road (Luke 10:25–37). Indeed, Jesus will extend the commandment to loving one's enemies (Matt 5:43–44). In the context of James where he reminds them that God has chosen the poor to inherit the kingdom, the royal law of the king, Jesus, is to love one's neighbor. And in the context of James, one's neighbor refers to the poor and vulnerable among them. As in Jas 1:25, there is a focus on doing the law. The law is not just something to be understood with the mind but rather is a way of life to be practiced. Those who fulfill the law of loving their neighbor are commended for their activity with the observation that they do well; in other words, they have acted in accordance with the standard set up by the law.

James and his audience both agree on the importance of the law of love, but verse 9 shows that James has set them up for reproof. If they are showing favoritism, then they are not practicing the law of love and are identified forcefully as those who "practice sin," as people who transgress against the law. Leviticus 19:15 specifically forbids showing partiality to the rich or the poor, but James at most alludes to that particular commandment in the context of focusing on the overarching law of love. Those who practice partiality are convicted by the law—they are identified as those who

76. Laws 1993: 108.
77. Davids 1982: 114.
78. Allison 2013: 402.

have disobeyed the law and rejected its claims on their actions. Verse 10 provides evidence that demonstrates that breaking one of the commandments involves being liable for the whole law. Peter Davids notes that this is a type of truism and adds, "Although penalties may vary, one is counted a criminal no matter which particular section of the code one may have broken."[79] It's a way of indicating that every commandment matters. But James's point is more than the idea that the law matters. Rather, he indicates that those who commit themselves to a way of life in line with God's law are guilty of violating that law even if they only break one of God's commandments. Scot McKnight says, "James has argued . . . for the final culpability for everyone and anyone who breaks even one commandment—and we are on sure grounds to think that James believed that each person in the community he addresses had done that."[80]

Verse 11 gives a second piece of evidence to support James's reproof that showing favoritism means that they are guilty of breaking God's law of love. God is the author or source of the law. Every commandment is set in place by God. James illustrates this with two of the ten commandments: do not commit adultery (Exod 20:14) and do not murder (Exod 20:13). Adultery will be alluded to further in Jas 4:4 when the audience are addressed as adulteresses. And murder describes the actions of the rich in James 5:6. Jewish interpretation of the ten commandments divided them into two parts—commandments aimed at loving God and commandments aimed at loving one's neighbor.[81] Here, these two commandments are probably cited because they fall at the beginning of the section that was commonly seen as guiding love of neighbor. The point that James is making is that the same divine source is behind all of the commandments, and it is no good to avoid one while committing the other. While the community is absolved of the charge that they are sleeping around with other people's spouses, they are accused of committing murder. This raises the question of whether James is referring to murder literally or figuratively. On the one hand, neglecting the poor as they are described as doing in 2:15–16, can ultimately lead to death as those without daily necessities such as food and shelter may be weakened and die. On the other hand, other NT texts such as Matt 5:21–22 associate "murder" with internal anger at a brother or sister and with insulting, slanderous speech towards others. The theme of speech has already

79. Davids 1982: 117.
80. McKnight 2011: 217.
81. Allison 2013: 415.

been introduced in James 1 and will continue to be a theme in James 2. Both the treatment of the poor and the intent of the heart will continue to be important themes in the book of James. In either case, those who fail to keep the law have become transgressors against the law. The language of "transgressor" was already used in 2:9 and James now concludes his argument that those who show favoritism are guilty of not living by the law of love. Their failure in this regard makes them a wrongdoer before the law, those who disregard God as the author of the law.

Considering this, James instructs them to speak and act as those who are about to be judged by the law of freedom.[82] The focus on both speech and action makes this a broad instruction about living a life that is fully committed to the law of love in word and deed. The commitment to the law of love takes place with the awareness that judgment is imminent. Most likely the reference is to God's judgment on the last day. This theme of God as the judge and final judgment is developed further in Jas 4:11–12 and 5:9. James ends this section with a pithy saying that sums up his understanding of the law of love. When the judgment comes, there is no mercy for the one who does not practice mercy. Mercy triumphs over judgment. God's mercy and love are intertwined. The Torah describes God as showing mercy to those that love God and keep the commandments (Exod 20:6; Deut 5:10). Allison notes that "loving one's neighbor means showing mercy to the poor, and showing mercy to the poor means loving one's neighbor."[83] In other words, mercy and love are joined together. Scot McKnight adds, "The messianic community is to speak and act toward the poor and marginalized in light of the judgment because the judgment will not show mercy to those who do not show mercy. This negative warrant is followed . . . by the alternative, a glimmer of hope and optimism: 'Mercy triumphs over judgment.' That is, if they become merciful toward the poor, they will escape the judgment."[84] God's mercy on the day of judgment is directed towards those who practice mercy. And, at the very least, there is the underlying suggestion that this community should be a community that imitates God by practicing mercy towards the most vulnerable. As the community confronts the problem of favoritism, the final saying encourages both the practice of mercy and an awareness of God's forthcoming judgment. The final phrase, "Mercy triumphs over judgment," leaves open the question of whose mercy James

---

82. See the commentary on Jas 1:25 for further discussion of "the law of freedom."
83. Allison 2013: 419.
84. McKnight 2011: 222.

is talking about. On the one hand, God is repeatedly identified as a God of mercy, and this may be James's meaning here. But Moo makes a very important point when he writes:

> But the "mercy" that James has been referring to in this context is human mercy, not God's (v. 12). We therefore think it more likely that he is making a point about the way in which the mercy we show toward others shows our desire to obey the law of the kingdom and, indirectly therefore, of a heart made right by the work of God's grace. The believer, in himself, will always deserve God's judgment: conformity to the "royal law" is never perfect, as it must be (vv. 10–11). But our merciful attitude and actions will count as evidence of the presence of Christ within us. And it is on the basis of this union with the one who perfectly fulfilled the law for us that we can have confidence of vindication at the judgment.[85]

Perhaps James is deliberately ambiguous, thereby inviting the reader to contemplate the mercy of God while calling the believer to merciful action.

Fusing the Horizons

At the heart of Jas 2:1–13 is the law of love: "Love your neighbor as yourself." This was the way of life promoted by Jesus. Such love explicitly forbids showing favoritism to those with power and status while disregarding or mistreating those whom the world perceives as having lower status. Indeed, it is the lowly and humble throughout James who find themselves exalted and chosen by God. Those who wish to have friendship with God will find practical ways to align themselves with the vulnerable. It can be tempting to use the excuse "everyone sins" to avoid the call on the church to show particular mercy to those among us who are most vulnerable. But the church should never be content with the idea that sin is a normal part of the Christian life. Instead, Christians are encouraged to recognize that the divine source of the law of love invites us to imitate God's mercy in our own acts of mercy. This can begin with the recognition that expensive clothes or ragged clothes neither determine the character of the one who wears them nor the relationship of the person to God. It begins by working to reject favoritism in the midst of the church. This is the difficult work of welcoming those who are not like us and helping them to find a place among the people of God where they can experience the love of God by being loved

---

85. Moo 2000: 119.

Commentary

as the neighbors God has brought to us. And the law of love can extend more fully through what John Wesley following Jesus referred to as "works of mercy," such as feeding the hungry, caring for the sick, visiting those in prison, and caring for the daily needs of the poor. Such works of mercy demand that the church have its eyes open to the needs of those around them and to the ways in which the church can come alongside those in need without stealing the very agency and voice of those in need.[86] Part of loving one's neighbors is helping those neighbors thrive in ways that recognize and facilitate the gifting God has given them. The church should be known as people who pursue wholeness with an integrity that practices love and mercy towards others.

---

86. Corbett and Fikkert 2009.

James

The Synergy of Faith and Works (James 2:14–26)

James 2:14–26: What is the benefit, my brothers and sisters, if someone says he has faith, but it is not accompanied by works? That faith is not able to save him, is it? (15) If a brother or sister is naked and lacking daily food, (16) and someone among you says to them, "Go in peace, be warmed and be filled," but does not give to them the things that are necessary for life, what is the benefit? (17) In the same way also faith by itself, if it is not accompanied by works, is dead.

(18) But someone will say, "you have faith, and I have works." Show me your faith apart from works, and I will show you my faith from my works. (19) You believe that God is one, you do well; the demons also believe and tremble.

(20) Do you want to know, O foolish man, that faith apart from works is worthless? (21) Was not Abraham our father justified by works when he offered up Isaac his son on the altar? (22) You see that his faith worked together with his works and by these works his faith was completed (23) and the scripture was fulfilled that says, "And Abraham believed God, and it was counted to him for righteousness" and he was called a friend of God. (24) See by works a man was justified and not by faith alone. (25) And likewise also was not Rahab the prostitute justified by works when she received the messengers and sent them away by another road? (26) For just as the body apart from the spirit[87] is dead, so also faith apart from works is dead.

James 2:14–26 relates to the material that came before. It has a parallel structure, it continues to develop the topic of "faith," which is mentioned throughout the chapter (vv. 1, 5, 14, 17, 18, 19, 20, 22, 23, 24, 26), and it continues to draw on illustrations related to the treatment of the poor. The chart below shows parallels between the structure of the two halves of James 2.

---

87. The Greek word *pneuma* can refer to both "spirit" and "breath." Most English translations choose "spirit" at this point (e.g., NRSV, NIV, ESV), but "breath" is also possible (NLT).

Commentary

James 2:1–13	James 2:14–26
Begins with a statement about *faith* and prejudice (v. 1)	Begins with two questions about *faith* and works (v. 14)
Includes a hypothetical illustration: the rich man and the poor man (vv. 2–4)	Includes a hypothetical illustration: the poorly clothed and hungry (vv. 15–16)
Ends with a pointed question: "Have you not become judges with evil thoughts?" (v. 4)	Ends with a pointed question: "What is the good of this?" (v. 16)
Provides an argument with evidence from the OT (vv. 8–11) in response to the initial question (vv. 5–13)	Provides an argument with evidence from the OT (vv. 21–25) in response to the initial questions (vv. 17–26)

In Jas 2:14–26, James makes the argument that faith and works necessarily go together and that right belief alone is insufficient for salvation. James supports this argument in three stages. First, in verses 14–17, James shows that faith without works of mercy towards the poor has no benefit for a person's salvation. Second, in verses 18–19, James shows that faith without works is the same as the faith of demons. Third, in verses 20–25, James shows that the forefathers and foremothers of the faith experienced salvation (justification) when they joined faith and works. James wraps up his argument by restating the thesis of Jas 2:14–26. Namely, "Faith apart from works is dead." Of course, one cannot read this portion of James without thinking about what Paul has to say about faith and works, especially since there seems to be disagreement between Paul's understanding of the relationship between faith and works and James's understanding. This commentary will examine the relationship between Paul and James and their understanding of faith and works in a short excursus at the end of the section.

Faith without Works is Dead (James 2:14–17)

James 2:14–17 begins with two questions. The first asks what advantage a person derives from faith that is not accompanied by works. To which the expected answer is "none." James adds a second question which gives further context to the first question. He asks, "That faith is not able to save him, is it?" The Greek (*mē*) clearly indicates that the answer to the second question is, "No, it cannot." What advantage is a person trying to gain by faith without works? The advantage, the benefit, the goal spoken of in the second question is salvation.[88] And James clearly indicates that faith separated from works cannot save. The meaning of the word faith (*pistis*) in the New Testament has been much debated in scholarly circles over the last fifty years. The Greek word *pistis* can be translated as "faith," "belief," "faithfulness," or "trust."[89] In English, we often understand these words differently so that "faith" or "trust" has a heart component to its meaning while "belief" is often seen as a cognitive word that denotes what we think about something. Scot McKnight describes the faith discussed in Jas 2:14–17 this way, "'Faith' evidently means—for the one with this kind of faith—'confessional' faith in God as one and Jesus as the Messiah as sufficient for redemption but not necessarily accompanied by deeds of mercy toward the marginalized."[90] In other words, this faith described here in James is about what one says about one's beliefs but not about the actions that accompany those beliefs.

But what "works" or actions is James referring to? In verses 15–16, James lays out a scenario in which there is a brother or a sister who is lacking clothing and hungry and a member of the congregation ("one of you") tells them to "go in peace, be warmed and filled" and doesn't give the needy person anything to sustain their daily needs. Verse 16 then ends with the question, "What benefit is that?" No one has benefited—neither the needy brother or sister nor the member of the congregation who has not joined faith and works together. While verses 15–16 point to concrete acts of feeding and clothing the poor, these actions are based on the "law of love" already laid out in Jas 2:8. Ultimately, "works" are the concrete activities that demonstrate love for one's neighbor. The Torah laid out lists of such activities. For example, Isa 58:6 lists the kinds of activities God approves of as part of the fast that he calls.

> Is not this the fast that I choose:
> to loose the bonds of injustice,
> to undo the thongs of the yoke,
> to let the oppressed go free,
> and to break every yoke?

---

88. McKnight 2011: 227.

89. Note that BDAG, 820, in ref. to Jas 2:14ab, 17, 18abc, 20, 22b, 24, 26 describes "*faith* as fidelity to Christian teaching. This point of view calls for εργα [works] as well as the kind of πιστις [faith] that represents only one side of true piety." It is worth pointing out that BDAG gives no other examples of such a usage in the NT.

90. McKnight 2011: 229.

> Is it not to share your bread with the hungry,
> and bring the homeless poor into your house;
> when you see the naked, to cover them,
> and not to hide yourself from your own kin?

Or another example, from Ezek 18:5–9 (emphasis added):

> If a man is righteous and does what is lawful and right—if he does not eat upon the mountains or lift up his eyes to the idols of the house of Israel, does not defile his neighbor's wife or approach a woman during her menstrual period, does not oppress anyone, but restores to the debtor his pledge, commits no robbery, *gives his bread to the hungry and covers the naked with a garment*, does not take advance or accrued interest, withholds his hand from iniquity, executes true justice between contending parties, follows my statutes, and is careful to observe my ordinances, acting faithfully—such a one is righteous; he shall surely live, says the Lord God.

Both prophetic texts enumerate a variety of "good works" that the righteous person engages. Other examples from the Old Testament could be joined with extra-biblical Jewish literature to make the point that caring for the poor and the marginalized was a crucial component of the good works to which the people of God were called. Jesus himself will sum up the law and the prophets with the two great commandments to "love the Lord your God with all your heart, soul, mind, and strength" and "to love your neighbor as yourself" (Mark 12:28–34). Throughout this passage, James will assert that "confessional belief" without action is not saving faith. Scot McKnight bluntly writes, "Most Protestants do not believe this today."[91]

James begins to answer his pointed questions by painting a small scenario in 2:15–16. There is a "brother or sister" who does not have sufficient clothing or food. It is unusual to note that the needy person may be either male or female, especially since Greek uses masculine plural words (*anthropoi, adelphoi*) to refer to people of both genders. James does this earlier when he addresses "the brothers" in Jas 1:16, 19; 2:1. In my translation of those verses, "brothers and sisters" is used to show the inclusivity of the masculine plural. Here, "brother and sister" shows that compassion extends to anyone, regardless of their gender. James Allison notes that women may have been more likely to be in need and refers back to the instruction

---

91. McKnight 2011: 229.

to visit widows in Jas 1:27.[92] As brothers and sisters, these needy people are members of the congregation. The text does not tell us where the member of the congregation encounters this brother or sister. In the ancient world, especially in cities and towns, people often lived much closer together than we do now (one of the impacts of the automobile!), and wealthy, poor, and those between all encountered each other regularly during their lives. As one example, one might think of the story of the rich man and Lazarus with Lazarus literally lying, apparently homeless, at the gates of the rich man (Luke 16:19–31). And from archaeology we have learned that the homes of the rich might literally be among living spaces used by those with far fewer resources. While James sees the poor as members of the congregation, he also envisions at least some people within the congregation having enough resources to be able to meet the needs of those who lack food and clothing. But in this particular case, the needy are sent away with only words. They are told to "go in peace." In the Old Testament, "peace" (*shalom*) refers to health, wholeness, and being well.[93] But here, the needy are not sent away with things that actually might bring them help—clothing to warm themselves or food to feed their hunger—but rather with words that are made meaningless by the lack of action accompanying them.

James sums up this section with a pithy and memorable encapsulation of his thesis: "Faith by itself, if it is not accompanied by works, is dead." When James declares that this kind of faith, faith not joined with works, is dead, he is saying that this faith is "so morally or spiritually deficient as to be in effect dead," lifeless.[94] Faith that is dead has no capacity to save. Salvation has already been described in James as originating with the Creator who gives birth to humanity and makes their redemption possible by the word of truth (1:18). Believers are invited to receive that saving word (1:21). Part of receiving is both listening (1:19) and doing (1:22). In this portion of James, doing works accompanied by faith is emphasized once again.

> *The nature of works in James:* For those who are Protestants, reading James can raise some significant questions. After all, the bedrock of Protestant belief is salvation by grace through faith alone. Ephesians 2:8–9 clearly indicates that salvation is a gift from God and that it is not a result of works. Similarly, Paul writes in Gal 2:16a, "Yet we know that a

---

92. Allison 2013: 463.
93. BDB, 1022.
94. BDAG, 667.

Commentary

person is justified not by the works of the law but through faith in Jesus Christ." And in Rom 4:1–5 Paul makes the argument that Abraham was justified by faith and not by works. And Paul uses the very same quotation that James uses to support his claim about Abraham! Readers rightly ask, how are we to reconcile the message of James ("faith without works is dead") and the message of Paul ("salvation is by grace through faith alone")?

Here, it is helpful to remember a number of things about the writings of James and Paul. First, these books are written to different audiences. James wrote to Jews. Paul wrote to gentiles. It seems likely that James was writing to a group who seemed to think that believing the right things was all that mattered. Meanwhile, Paul seems to have encountered people who thought that being Jewish and keeping Jewish regulations related to circumcision, diet, and holy days mattered for salvation. These different concerns led to different emphases for these two writers. Second, it seems that James and Paul may have understood "works" differently. James sees "works" as good things that are done as evidence of true faith. Paul sometimes uses the language "works of the law" (e.g., Gal 2), which can refer to the status markers that marked people as Jewish, such as circumcision, dietary laws, and Sabbath keeping. In this understanding, Paul is indicating that one's status does not provide entry into salvation. Third, Paul also talks about good works as the outflow of faith. For example, in the Ephesians passage that seems to provide such strong evidence for salvation by faith alone, Paul goes on to write, "For we are . . . created in Christ Jesus for good works, which God prepared beforehand to be our way of life." In other words, Paul also sees good works as part of the life of faith. In fact, many of Paul's letters end with sections that teach the Christian community about the way they should live in light of the good news about Jesus (e.g., Romans 12–13; 1 Thess 4–5). Finally, it's important to remember that in the first century, Jewish interpretation of the Scripture was diverse. There was not a single, correct way to read, use, and understand the Scriptures. Instead, these were applied as the interpreter felt that they were relevant to the argument. This helps to explain the different uses of Genesis and the patriarch, Abraham, by James and Paul. While Protestants, especially following Martin Luther, have emphasized Paul and the message of salvation as a gift from God. It is important that we also emphasize the voice of James and hear his message that belief needs to be joined with action. In James's message those actions are particularly concerned with care for

> the widow, the orphan, and others in need—those who are hungry, who need shelter, who need clothing.

Faith in the One God (James 2:18-19)

These verses are an objection to the statement that faith apart from works is dead. The argument begins, "But someone will say." This picks up on the "someone" in verse 14: "If someone says he has faith . . ." Now, this someone paints a picture in which one person has faith ("you have faith") and another person has works ("and I have works").[95] James associates with the voice of the "I" and commands, "Show me your faith apart from works." His assumption is that it is impossible to demonstrate faith without accompanying good works. In contrast, he claims that his good works will demonstrate his faith. Once again, as in Jas 2:14-17, faith and works are seen as inextricably intertwined. Finally, he goes on to say, "You believe," and he provides the content of what the person believes. They believe that God is one. This assertion draws on the Jewish *shema*, the ancient daily acknowledgment of God prayed by Jews throughout the centuries. The *shema* is found in Deut 6:4. In that context, Moses has just finished reiterating the commandments that God gave to the people—commandments about putting God first and commandments about treating one's neighbors rightly. This ends with the proclamation, "Hear, O Israel: The Lord our God, the Lord is one" (NIV). This is immediately followed by the instruction to "love the Lord your God with all your heart, and with all your soul, and with all your might" (Deut 6:5). In other words, the recognition that God is the one true God is followed by the commandment to love him. This acknowledgment of God and the instruction to love him wholeheartedly comes after instructions to put

95. This passage has long been acknowledged as presenting interpretive challenges. Martin Dibelius (writing in 1964), Luke Timothy Johnson (writing in 1995), and James Allison (writing in 2013) each indicate that this is either one of the most difficult passages in the NT or in the book of James. Questions arise about who is speaking ("someone says"), the extent of their speech (e.g., where the quotation marks should be placed), and who the pronouns refer to ("you" and "I"). The debate around these issues can be seen by comparing English translations, which put the quotation marks in different places (NASB and NIV are two examples). Critical commentaries such as those listed above and below can be consulted for lengthy discussions of these issues. This commentary follows Johnson, McKnight, Moo, and others in arguing that an opponent here presents a contrast between two people: one with faith ("you") and one with works ("I"). James then responds by taking up the "I" of the person with works.

Commentary

God first and to live in ways that demonstrate love, honor, and respect towards one's neighbor (e.g., not killing, stealing, coveting, bearing false witness, etc.). James indicates that the person who has faith affirms the creedal beliefs that have been central to faith in Israel's God. He even affirms that the person who asserts this belief does well.

But then, he delivers a slap in the face. There is nothing commendable about their faith. They are only doing as well as the demons! Their faith is the same faith that the demons have. In other words, the demons also know that God is the one true God. And they have a response . . . they tremble or shudder on account of their knowledge of the one true God.

OT Examples Demonstrating Faith without Works is Dead (James 2:20–26)

James now continues to address the "someone" of verse 18. He asks the person who asserts the possibility that faith does not need to be joined with works whether he or she really wants to know that these two things need to be joined. Since James then refers to that person as someone "devoid of intellectual, moral, or spiritual value,"[96] the assumption is that the person really doesn't want to know. In other words, he or she would rather hold to their position than really know the evidence from the Old Testament that shows that faith and works are inseparably conjoined.

The first example that James draws on is Abraham, the great patriarch from which Israel descended and whom both Jews and Christians esteem as a righteous person. For example, "Abraham was perfect in all his deeds with the Lord, and well-pleasing in righteousness all the days of his life" (Jub. 23:10). This was the lens through which first-century Jews viewed Abraham. James introduces his example from Abraham's life with the rhetorical question, "Was not Abraham our father justified by his works?" The question expects the answer, "Yes, he was" (Greek: *ou*). In this verse, James alludes to the sacrifice of Isaac recounted in Genesis 22.

> *Questioning The Sacrifice of Isaac:* The Genesis story has long presented an interpretive challenge for both Jewish and Christian interpreters. The most pressing questions readers ask about this story is why would the God who condemns child sacrifice ask Abraham to sacrifice his son.

96. BDAG, 539.

> Or, some might ask more directly how a loving God could ask a father to murder his child? Jon Levenson has responded to these questions by reminding readers that in both Jewish and Christian interpretations throughout the centuries, Abraham has been seen as the paradigm of someone who responds to God with faithfulness, obedience, and submission in the face of the most difficult test of all.[97] Seeing Abraham's action as immoral has been a particular strand of the history of interpreting this story that is influenced by the enlightenment, which proposed a universal ethic for humanity that was determined by human rationality. This understanding of ethics was intended to displace an ethic based on relationship with God and God's commandments. In the biblical text, the test that God sets for Abraham is rooted in the relationship between Abraham and God and in Abraham's response to God's commandment. Abraham is not a murderer. The language of killing is not used in this text. Instead, this is the language of sacrifice, of making an offering of something of value to God. It is Abraham's very *love* for Isaac that makes following God's instruction a sacrifice.[98] Levenson then notes, "*In the biblical text, sacrifice is not deemed unethical or irrational*, and it requires no more of an act of faith to adhere to sacrificial demands than it requires to adhere to ethical demands. . . . The point is that in ancient Israel . . . sacrifice . . . was not regarded as an offense to reason or a departure from universal custom."[99] Contemporary questions about how God could ask for such a sacrifice are derived more from our own context than from the context of ancient Israel.

In this difficult and famous story from the end of Abraham's life, God tests Abraham one final time. God has repeatedly tested Abraham throughout their relationship, and often the pattern of that test has been that God makes a promise and then gives Abraham an instruction to carry out. But in this final test, God gives an instruction without a promise, "Take your son, your only son Isaac, whom you love, and go to the land of Moriah, and offer him there as a burnt offering on one of the mountains that I shall show you" (Gen 22:2). The next morning, Abraham gets up and proceeds to do as God has instructed him. It is only as he is raising the knife to sacrifice his son that an angel stops him, and God provides a ram to be sacrificed

---

97. Levenson 1998: 260.
98. Levenson 1998: 269.
99. Levenson 1998: 271 (emphasis original).

in Isaac's place. Then, God affirms his promise to Abraham—the promise of relationship with God, of land, and of descendants.[100] This is the event from Abraham's life that James alludes to in verse 21 when claiming that Abraham was justified by his works. While one might ask how Abraham's sacrifice of Isaac was a work, it seems clear that James equates "work" with action. In other words, creedal belief alone is not sufficient to demonstrate faith. Faith is demonstrated when someone acts as a result of faith. In verses 22–24 James provides further commentary on the narrative of the binding of Isaac and how it relates to faith being joined together with works. James makes four claims: (1) faith was at work alongside Abraham's works; (2) faith was completed (made perfect) by works; (3) Scripture was fulfilled (by his works); and (4) he was called a friend of God.[101] These four points lead to James's conclusion in verse 24: a person is justified by works and not by faith alone.

Before turning to verses 22–24, we need to look in more depth at verse 21. The word "justified" is only used three times (vv. 21, 24, 25) in James. For Protestants who have grown up with an emphasis on Paul, "justification" refers to the way God places those who trust in him in right relationship with God and enables them to be found righteous at the last judgment. While this is Paul's language of salvation, James has spoken of salvation differently. James describes God giving birth to his people (1:18) and implanting his word in them (1:21). Now, in the context of the discussion about faith and works, James uses the language "justified." The question this raises is whether James uses "justify" in the same way as Paul or whether James uses it differently. James has already been talking about salvation (cf. v. 14), and now he asks whether Abraham is justified by his works. There are several ways one can understand the meaning of "Abraham was justified." Vlachos lists the possibilities this way: (1) it refers to validating the reality of Abraham's faith; (2) it refers to Abraham being made morally right with God; or (3) it refers to being declared righteous at the final judgment.[102] Many commentators argue for the idea that in this context "justification" refers to God's validation of the authenticity of Abraham's faith.[103] However, this is not the most common meaning of the word in the Old Testament and in some parts of the New Testament where it refers to "the ultimate

---

100. Clines 1997.
101. Allison 2013: 494.
102. Vlachos 2013: 95–96.
103. Davids 1982: 128.

vindication of the believer in the judgment . . . based on . . . the things that person has done."[104] Yet other NT passages refer to being made right with God by being brought into right relationship with God (e.g., Rom 3:23–26). James has already been talking about salvation since 2:14, where he asks whether faith without works is capable of saving. James continues to assert that faith and works are necessary components of salvation. When God justified Abraham because of his works, God was declaring that Abraham was righteous because of his obedience. "One could say that God declared what Abraham demonstrated."[105] Dale Allison goes on to note, "James does not counter one extreme—justification by faith alone—with another extreme—justification by works alone. He instead stakes out the middle ground: faith and deeds are necessary."[106]

James now offers commentary on his allusion to the binding of Isaac. First, he addresses the audience with the words "you see," and then lays out four things that he anticipates are clear to his audience. First, they see that "faith worked together with his works." In other words, this is not about works alone. Rather, faith aids the doing of works. Once again, James sees faith and works as intimately intertwined. Second, they see that "faith was brought to completion (or perfection) by his works." Belief may be the initiating force for works, but without works, faith is incomplete. Faith is only one side of a necessary whole. Note, however, that James never argues that works alone are sufficient. Instead, the two always go together. Faith aids the doing of works, and works brings faith to a state of completion. Third, James's audience can see his point that the binding of Isaac is a fulfillment of the scriptural citation found in Gen 15:6. Luke Timothy Johnson puts it this way, "He states that the *graphē* [Scripture] declaring Abraham righteous in Gen 15:6 was fulfilled by the *deed* that Abraham performed by offering his son Isaac. This is finding a prophecy/fulfillment pattern within Torah itself."[107] James refers to the work (the binding of Isaac) before quoting the passage that refers to Abraham's faith. James knows that the passage about Abraham's faith comes before the binding of Isaac, so he sees the binding of Isaac as the fulfillment of that passage.

The passage that James cites comes from Gen 15. In this chapter God promises Abraham that his reward will be very great, but Abraham's

---

104. Moo 2000: 136.
105. Allison 2013: 483.
106. Allison 2013: 484.
107. Johnson 1995: 243.

response to that promise is to remind God that he has no heir. Then God tells Abraham that he will have a son, one who is born from his own seed. Not only that, but Abraham will have many, many descendants. After God has made this promise, the text says, "And he believed the LORD and the LORD reckoned it to him as righteousness" (v. 6). This is the faith that James points to, but James does not see that faith as being fulfilled until Abraham is willing to offer Isaac on the altar. It is one thing to *say* that you believe God, and it is another thing to *act* on that faith. Abraham acted on his faith in God's promise when he was willing to offer the very son that had been promised to him on the altar. In this way, his action shows that he truly trusts God. This understanding of the relationship between Gen 15:6 and the binding of Isaac is not unusual in the first century. One example of this can be seen in 1 Macc 2:52, which asks, "Was not Abraham found faithful when tested, and it was reckoned to him as righteousness?" The reference to testing can be understood as the story of the binding of Isaac, where God tests Abraham with the instruction to sacrifice his son, and the reference to being reckoned as righteous refers to Genesis 15. In other words, Jewish readers would not have thought that it was unusual for James to understand the binding of Isaac as a fulfillment of the Scripture in which Abraham believed God.

Verse 23 wraps up with the declaration that Abraham was called a friend of God. Luke Timothy Johnson notes that in the Greco-Roman world friendship emphasized "the essential equality and unity of friends."[108] These are people who share life together and see things in the same way. Abraham was considered a friend of God throughout Jewish literature. "For he was found faithful, and was recorded on the heavenly tablets as the friend of God" (Jub. 19:9b) is just one example of Abraham as a friend of God.[109] Similarly, from an early Christian document 1 Clem. 10:1, "Abraham, who was called the friend, was found faithful in becoming obedient to the words of God." This view of Abraham most likely derived from the conversation God had with Abraham over the destruction of Sodom in Gen 18 in which God decided not to hide his intentions from Abraham. This choice to share intimately with Abraham was one aspect of the relationship that showed that God considered Abraham his friend. The use of the word "friend" here points ahead to Jas 4:4 and the observation that the one who is a friend of the world is an enemy of God. James now summarizes and reiterates his

---

108. Johnson 1995: 244.
109. Charles 1913.

argument about Abraham's faith and works as seen in his declaration of faith in Gen 15 and his binding of Isaac in Gen 22. He writes, "You see that a person is justified by works and not by faith alone." Ultimately, James's point is that both faith and works are necessary. Faith alone is insufficient, and works without faith do not save. Both are needed.

Verse 25 now offers a second example from Scripture. This time James draws on the narrative of Rahab found in Josh 2:1–24 and 6:22–25. In this famous story, two spies are rescued when Rahab hides them from the king's men who are seeking them. She then declares all that she has heard about the Lord and asks them to spare her life. Next, she helps them escape out of her window and tells them what roads to take to avoid those who are searching for them. Like Abraham, Rahab joins her faith to her action. Her belief that "The LORD your God is indeed God in heaven above and on earth below" (Josh 2:11) is joined with her action in choosing to harbor the spies, to protect them by lying to government authorities, to enable them to escape, and to direct them on how to return safely to the Israelite camp. Jonathan Edwards says of this example, "Had Rahab the harlot said to the spies, 'I believe God is yours, and Canaan is yours, but dare not show you any kindness,' her faith had been dead and unactive, and would not have justified her."[110] Indeed, in many ways Rahab is the exact opposite of Abraham—a woman, a prostitute, and a gentile. Yet, her actions are also described as justifying actions by James. Both the forefathers and the foremothers joined faith and works together and experienced right relationship with God through that joining.

James gives one final illustration as he wraps up his argument. Namely, a body without the spirit is dead. Spirit here refers to that which animates the body, the breath.[111] A body without breath is simply a corpse. In the same way, faith (here, analogous to the body) without works (the animating spirit) is also dead.

Fusing the Horizons

Protestants can spend lifetimes, indeed centuries, debating the relationship between faith, works, and justification, but it is clear from both James and Paul that good works are an expected component of trust in God and faithful response to the new life that has been made available by God's gift. In

---

110. Edwards quoted in Allison 2013: 499.
111. Martin 1988: 98.

James, these good works are particularly focused on care for the poor, for those who lack what is necessary for daily survival. The church has a long history from its very inception of caring for the needy among them and even those in need who were not followers of Jesus. In the book of Acts, we see the church meeting the needs of widows (Acts 6) and providing clothing for the needy (Acts 9:36–42). The early church continued this practical care for the needy among them. And in the first centuries of the church Roman writers themselves would argue that it was the care Christians showed for the poor that won people over to the faith.[112] The church's care for the poor has continued to be an important aspect of the faith through the centuries. Today, churches continue these practices of care for the poor in a variety of ways: food pantries, free charity shops, rent relief, and other practical help.

There's also another side to the coin when considering the message of James chapter 2. Elsa Tamez, a Latin American scholar, in her book *The Scandalous Message of James* reminds us that this chapter reads quite differently when read from the perspective of the poor. For the poor, this chapter contains a lot of good news. They are the ones that God has chosen to be inheritors of the kingdom (2:5). They are the ones whom those with resources should love as neighbors (2:8, 15–16). They are the ones who should be regarded without prejudice (2:2–4). For those who are not poor, this good news may be quite uncomfortable for several reasons. First, it may seem quite unfair that God chooses based on the vulnerability caused by poor socio-economic realities. Second, often the poor are blamed for their circumstances. *If that person had made better choices; if that person practiced self-control; if . . .* James places no blame on the poor for their circumstances. Instead, it is quite clear that part of their situation is caused by the wealthy—those who drag them into court and oppress them. This will be further fleshed out in Jas 5:1–6. Those who practice works of mercy, who care for the poor, needy, and vulnerable in this world, have an opportunity to participate in the good news that God proclaims to those who are usually on the margins of society.

---

112. Wright 1913: 338.

James

The Untamable Tongue Capable of Great Destruction (James 3:1–12)

James 3:1–12: Not many of you should become teachers, my brothers and sisters, since you know that we will receive a greater judgment. (2) For we all stumble in many ways. If anyone does not stumble in speech, that one is a perfect person who is also able to hold in check the whole body. (3) Now, when we put bits into the mouths of horses so that they obey us, we guide their whole body also. (4) Consider also boats which are so large and driven by strong winds yet are guided by the smallest rudder wherever the will of the pilot desires. (5) So also the tongue is a small member but boasts great things. Behold! A small spark kindles a great forest fire.

(6) And the tongue is a fire. The tongue is a world of unrighteousness setting itself among our members; it stains the whole body and sets on fire the course of human experience and is set on fire by Gehenna. (7) For every kind of both animals and birds, of both reptiles and sea creatures are being tamed and have been tamed by humans, (8) but no human is able to tame the tongue. It is a restless evil, full of deadly poison. (9) With it we bless the Lord and Father and with it we curse humans created according to the likeness of God; (10) out of the same mouth comes forth blessing and cursing. My brothers and sisters, these things ought not to be so. (11) Does a spring gush forth sweet and bitter water out of the same opening? (12) Is a fig tree able, my brothers and sisters, to produce olives, or is a vine able to produce figs? Neither does salty water produce sweet water.

In James 2 the focus was upon the necessity of both faith and works. The chapter began by showing that favoritism has no place within the Christian community. Indeed, such partiality violates the law of love that originates in the covenant that God made with Israel and is reiterated by Jesus himself. The chapter then continued by showing that true faith is demonstrated in the way Christians respond to the needs of others and live in obedience to God. Now, in James 3 the book begins to describe more fully the need for Christians to control their speech. The introduction of the topic of teachers and the tongue or speech seems quite abrupt, and some commentators have seen no relationship between this section of James and what has come before.[113] Others have argued that words are a form of action and/or that James is now developing a theme that he began in the first

---

113. Dibelius 1975: 182.

chapter of James. Douglas Moo takes both these positions and describes the relationship this way:

> First, the concern about "words" in this paragraph is loosely connected to the concern about "works" in 2:14–26; as Tasker puts it, "words are also works . . ." A movement from the importance of works to the crucial "work" of human speech is therefore a natural progression. Second, this long section on the problem of the tongue picks up James's identification of the control of the tongue as one of the clearest examples of "true religion" (1:26; cf. 1:19–20).[114]

We can also note that in James 2:12 the instruction given is "so speak and so act as those about to be judged by the law of freedom." James then immediately discussed "works," in other words, actions in 2:14–26. Now, he turns to the other item from 2:12, speech.

James continues speaking to the brothers and sisters scattered throughout the diaspora, and he instructs that not many of them should become teachers. He does not explicitly say why they shouldn't become teachers[115] but instead reminds them that teachers will receive a greater judgment. This judgment may come from both God and from other members of the community.[116] Teachers played an important role in the early Christian community. Paul lists teaching as one of the roles that God has given (1 Cor 12:28) in order to strengthen the ministry of the church (Eph 4:11). Sound and wise teaching was important to the continuation of Christianity. Teaching in the first century did not involve degrees and approval from institutions like our universities and seminaries but rather the capacity to expound on scripture (both the Old Testament and Christian teaching) for the benefit of the community. Although James does not explicitly indicate why someone should avoid becoming a teacher, there are several possible reasons. Teachers have greater responsibility to speak carefully and truthfully, and there is concern that some were speaking in irresponsible and unloving ways.[117] Some might aspire to be teachers because it gave greater power and social status within the community rather than becoming teachers in order to serve with humility.[118] Some scholars have thought that James is

---

114. Moo 2000: 147.
115. Allison 2013: 520.
116. Moore-Keish 2019: 119.
117. McKnight 2011: 268–69.
118. Davids 1989: 80.

issuing a warning against false teachers such as we see in books like Jude.[119] However, it isn't clear from the context what kind of false doctrine or false ethic these teachers are proposing and James is resisting. In light of this, it seems best to understand that James is warning the community generally, those he addresses as brothers and sisters, to be careful about desiring to become a teacher. The address itself is to the whole community and not specifically to teachers. Allison rightly makes the point that it would make no sense to tell teachers not to desire to be teachers.[120] And Moo indicates that "most commentators, without ignoring v. 1, nevertheless do not think that James is concerned only, or even especially, with teachers throughout the paragraph. They suggest that James singles out teachers at the outset because they provide a convenient 'jumping off point' for the general warning about the tongue."[121] In light of this, suggestions by other scholars that this whole section is addressed to teachers and that this section is about leadership in the church do not have the strongest support. Although the idea that "the tongue" refers to the teacher and that "the body" refers to the congregation is an interesting one, the evidence for this position from the text itself is not strong enough to clearly make that metaphorical move. The images that James works with can be interpreted without recourse to a metaphorical view of the body as the church (an idea developed in Paul but not laid out in James). Thus, this portion of James, like the rest of the book, is addressed to the whole audience and not simply a special group of "teachers" within that audience.

The first reason given in support of the directive that not many should desire to be teachers is because "you know that we will receive a greater judgment." James identifies himself among those who are teachers and reminds his audience that they already know that teachers will receive a greater judgment. This "greater judgment" most likely occurs at the end time and can be understood in two ways. It may refer to being judged by a stricter standard and the idea that more will be expected from those who carried great responsibility as leaders of the church. Those who lead are held to a higher standard because their leadership as teachers sets a moral example for the community they lead.[122] Or, "greater judgment" may refer

---

119. Martin 1988: 108.
120. Allison 2013: 519.
121. Moo 2000: 147.
122. Davids 1989: 81.

to receiving a harsher or heavier punishment, again, because more is expected of those who lead through their teaching.[123]

The second reason that they should not aspire to be teachers is because everyone stumbles—both teachers and all the members of the community. The word "stumble" may refer to minor errors or missteps in life or in speech and thus emphasizes how unlikely it is that anyone can avoid sin completely. It may also serve as a reminder that speech is one of the easiest areas in which to stumble. But James goes on to say that if speech could be mastered, then they would be perfect! McKnight notes, "When James speaks of a 'perfect' teacher in 3:2 . . . this person is a fully developed follower of Jesus's own teachings of the Torah as the Torah of loving God and loving others. The perfect teacher is one whose love shapes how he or she teaches and speaks of others. Indeed, the term speaks of maturity and completeness or, even better, of having arrived at the destined goal designed by God."[124] Such people, those who have been formed and shaped by God in such a way that they can control their speech, are also able to control their bodies. In 3:2–3, James reintroduces the metaphor of the bit and bridle which was already used in 1:26 to describe a person who was unable to control the tongue. That person's religious practices were described as useless (1:26). Now, the positive side of that metaphor is given. The bridle is part of the gear that allows the rider to guide the horse where she wills. That language of control and restraint is now applied to the person who has mastered the tongue. The one who masters the tongue, that one is a perfect person. It seems that these two statements in 3:2 stand in tension. The text indicates that we all stumble in many ways. In the very next sentence, the text indicates that if people do not make mistakes, they are perfect. This raises the question, "If we all stumble, does that mean perfection is out of reach?" We must remember that in James "perfection" does not refer to sinlessness but rather to maturity, to wholeness in one's character and life, especially as one grows in wisdom and friendship with God. When Patrick Hartin discusses wholeness and perfection in relationship to speech, he says, "Here the concept of integrity dominates. Those who always tell the truth are those who harmonize thought and speech. They conform to the way God has created them, by using speech to bless God and one another (3:9–10)."[125] Some have thought that some may be able to master the tongue.

123. Dibelius 1975: 182.
124. McKnight 2011: 275.
125. Hartin 1999: 152.

Others have thought such mastery is impossible. The analogies that follow point in both directions. On the one hand, there are positive analogies of the horse controlled by the bit and the ship guided by the pilot's hand on the rudder. On the other hand, there is an analogy of a fiery spark that leads to destruction. The tongue that is under control can guide the body in a good direction, but the tongue that is out of control is an agent of destruction. Like the bit and the rudder, the tongue is also a small thing in comparison to the whole. But despite its relative size, it boasts great things. While boasting is not necessarily negative, it is often connected to such sins as pride and arrogance in the Old Testament. In Psalm 12, the Psalmist asks the Lord to "cut off all flattering lips, the tongue that makes great boasts, those who say, 'with our tongues we will prevail; our lips are our own—who is our master?'" (vv. 3-4). And in the New Testament, other authors will speak of not boasting in one's own abilities as if one is able to save oneself but rather boasting in God alone (1 Cor 1:31). Since James will go on to associate the tongue with destructive fire, it is best to understand the boasting that is described here as negative, contrary to friendship with God, and driven by negative characteristics such as self-promotion, inordinate pride, and arrogance. Indeed, the next analogy is that a small spark can start a great forest fire. Just as those who live in the dry western states of the USA are keenly aware of the danger of sparks from something as small as a car backfire or a smoldering cigarette, so too the inhabitants of the first century were keenly aware of the danger of fire, both the kind of brush and forest fires described here as well as fires that burned through villages and cities. The tongue is compared to a small spark that can start a great destructive fire.

Fusing the Horizons

Teachers continue to play a significant role in the life of the church providing insight and interpretation of Scripture, giving guidance to the church in terms of doctrine and theology and leading in a variety of ways. James does not discourage the work of teaching, but he does warn those who would seek to be teachers about the responsibility they bear as people who use their speech to lead others. One of the things that is crucial in the church's identification of teachers is a focus on *both* the character of the teacher and the knowledge the teacher has. Those whose character has not been transformed by learning joy in the midst of testing and trials (1:2-4), by learning to resist temptation and receive God's word of truth (1:13-18), and by learning to be doers of the word (1:22–25) may need more time to grow before they enter into the work of teaching. This is particularly true when we understand that the church itself places higher expectations on its teachers and that teachers will experience greater judgment in the last times.

Perhaps James starts this section of the book with a focus on those who want to be teachers because he recognizes that this is a profession that centers around speech and communication. But he quickly turns his attention to the whole congregation. On the one hand, everyone stumbles. This is a reminder to be careful about judging others who have stumbled too harshly because we recognize our own shortcomings. At the same time, this is not an excuse to accept sin either in ourselves or in others. Immediately following the recognition that we all make mistakes comes the picture of the perfect person—a person able to control his or her speech, to speak with integrity and truthfulness. While Jewish and Greco-Roman moralists recommended strategies such as silence or being a person of few words in order to control the tongue, James gives no such advice here. Instead, we might think about the type of person that is envisioned in James 1–2: a person who asks God for wisdom, who receives God's gifts, who endures testing and temptation, who practices the word that has been heard, and who especially cares for the vulnerable. Such practices, especially if one does not boast about them, form the inner person and in this way shape the speech of believers. Likewise, speech that is directed towards asking God for wisdom (1:5), that avoids blaming God for hardship (1:13), that avoids prejudice and mistreatment of others (2:2–5), and that is accompanied by action (2:14–17) shapes the character of the person. Speech and action, action and speech—these two together shape the true character of the one who has received God's word and lives by it in both word and deed. But, as we read on in this chapter in James, it becomes clear that controlling one's speech is decidedly difficult.

Destructive Speech: (James 3:6–12)

After the three analogies of horse, ship, and fire, James moves to metaphor. The tongue or speech is equated with destructive fire. Some might point out that fire is not always a negative image. After all, the disciples were filled with the Holy Spirit when tongues of fire rested on them, and they were enabled to speak in many languages (Acts 2:1–4). However, the fire that is described in James has nothing holy about it. Instead, the descriptions that follow the connection between speech and fire indicate that the force that animates speech causes pollution, unrighteousness, and regular disruption to the ups and downs of life. In addition, the underlying destructive power of the tongue is derived from hell itself. In this portion of James there is little indication that the tongue and speech have a positive association.

Not only is the tongue a fire, but it is a world of unrighteousness. "The most common meaning of *kosmos* in the NT is 'world,' often with the nuance of the fallen, sinful world-system."[126] The inclination of the tongue is to draw on the wisdom of the world for its content—the kind of wisdom that says, "Get your own back"; "put down others in order to lift yourself up"; "only tell the truth when it's convenient"; "the most outrageous speech gets the most attention, and fame is all that matters"; or "staying true to your word is old-fashioned." This is without mentioning the patterns of abusive and oppressive speech that make up so much interaction in the world. The tongue has become its own unrighteous system, a system apart from God. When this small part is set among the whole body, that unrighteous system ends up spoiling the whole body. Again, remember that speech and deeds are intertwined for James: declarative faith is joined by action. When speech has become a world of unrighteousness, then the actions of the body are also informed by that speech. In this way the tongue's world of unrighteousness ends up staining the whole body. But this world of unrighteousness is not limited to staining the body. It is also described as literally "setting on fire the wheel of life." There is some debate about the meaning of this phrase. Some have argued that ideas about the cycle of birth and death from Buddhism may have infiltrated from the east and that the idea of a "wheel of life" refers to this.[127] This is a possibility. But in the context of James, the idea of the "wheel of life" may mean something more like the ups and downs of human experience.[128] In other words, over the course of a life, the tongue as a fiery world of unrighteousness impacts the daily realities of life. James wraps up this verse with the comment that the tongue is "set on fire by Gehenna." Gehenna refers to a valley south of Jerusalem. In the gospels, Gehenna (often translated "hell" in English Bibles) is the place of punishment and destruction (e.g., Matt 10:28; Mark 9:43). There are two ways to understand James's comment about the tongue being set on

---

126. Moo 2000: 157.
127. Allison 2013: 540.
128. Dibelius 1975: 198.

fire by hell. First, there has been a long tradition of understanding "hell" as the dwelling place of the devil and his cohort. In this understanding, the tongue, by being associated with hell, is associated with the demonic. Elsewhere in James, earthly wisdom is associated with the demonic (3:15) and his audience is told to resist the devil (4:7), so James clearly associates that which is opposed to God with demonic forces. Second, it is also possible to argue that the tongue being set on fire by hell is a reference to the destruction the tongue will suffer when it is judged. In other words, something along the lines of "the tongue itself will be lit up by the fires of hell." To put it another way, the very thing that has been destructively lighting on fire life itself will be justly judged when it is destroyed in the fires of hell.

Now James moves straight into hyperbole with the claim that every kind of creature (beast, bird, reptile, and sea creature) is being tamed and has been tamed by humans. This is an obvious overstatement since clearly not every kind of creature has been tamed by humans. The hyperbole is used to set up the contrast with verse 8. In contrast to the human capacity to tame every kind of creature, no human being can tame the tongue. This too is a hyperbolic statement that highlights James's negative view of the tongue. The tongue is a "restless evil." The same adjective that was used in 1:8 (*akatastatos*) is used here. There, it describes the one who doubts as unstable and is connected to the idea of being in two minds. Here it describes the evil of the tongue as something that is restless.

> The nature of this "restless evil" is not entirely clear. On the one hand, James might be reiterating how hard it is to control the tongue: it is, as Phillips paraphrases, "always liable to break out." On the other hand, James could be thinking of the "instability and lack of single-mindedness" that characterize the tongue. The former idea fits well with the emphasis on the difficulty of taming the tongue in vv. 7–8. But the latter anticipates the argument of vv. 9–12 and matches the other occurrence of the word in James.[129]

It is full of deadly poison. "Poison" can refer to the venom of poisonous snakes or to poison more generally. Here, it has a figurative meaning showing that words have the potential to destroy both ourselves and others.

James again presents a choice between "two ways," a way aligned with God and a way aligned with that which is earthly and devilish. There is no middle ground in James. That which is less than single-minded is impure. When James describes the tongue that is used both to bless God and to

---

129. Moo 2000: 163.

curse humans, he is laying out a scenario where the person uses the tongue in two opposing ways. Such doubleness is unstable and distant from God's wisdom (cf. Jas 1:7–8). To bless God is to praise him. The Psalmist repeatedly declares that he will bless the Lord (e.g., Pss 26:12; 34:1; 63:4) and blessing God was a common part of Jewish and early Christian worship. The identification of God as Father reflects the understanding that God is the Creator and Redeemer.[130] It is the use of the tongue for the language of praise followed by the use of the tongue for cursing humanity that James condemns. Moo writes, "The ancient curse was far more than abusive language; it called on God, in effect, to cut a person off from any possible blessing and to consign that person to Hell."[131] Similarly, McKnight notes, "Blessing and cursing have to do with life and death. As Prov 18:21 puts it, 'Death and life are in the power of the tongue,' or as Sir 28:12 has it, 'If you blow on a spark, it will glow; if you spit on it, it will be put out; yet both come out of your mouth.'"[132] This is not a simple prohibition against swearing. Rather, it is a reminder that the tongue that is set on fire by hell can spew forth hate and destruction. James 3:9 reminds us that any such hateful use of the tongue is a form of violence against people who have been made in the image of God. This takes the reader back to Gen 1:26, "Then God said, 'Let us make humankind in our image, according to our likeness.'" God's crowning work of creation was to make humanity in his image and give humanity the task of stewarding the creation.[133] When someone curses another human being, one is cursing God's creation. "Thus, the prohibition of cursing was aimed at those who struck out in anger (see Matt 5:21–26) against other Christians, especially when disputes flared up during internal squabbles. Such a practice could easily characterize those who are pictured as double-minded (1:7, 8), who manifest an attitude of partiality (2:4), and who accept the lopsided doctrine of faith without deeds."[134] In 3:10, the text clearly identifies a single source, the mouth, for two opposite things: blessing and cursing. James is clear. "These things ought not to be." James

---

130. McKnight 2011: 293.

131. Moo 2000: 163.

132. McKnight 2011: 291.

133. The end of Gen 1:26 "and let them have dominion" has often been misread in ways that have encouraged environmental destruction of both habitat and animals. But a better reading of the passage understands God as the great king who entrusts humanity as a lesser king with care for that which ultimately belongs to God. For further exploration of these issues see Richter 2020.

134. Martin 1988: 119.

turns to examples from nature to show how unnatural it is for two opposite things to come from one source. A spring only produces one kind of water. A fig tree only produces figs. An olive tree only produces olives. Salt water does not produce fresh water. The mouth that produces two kinds of things from one source is not associated with purity or wisdom but rather with the double-minded, unstable, earthly wisdom from below.

Fusing the Horizons

The tongue in James 3 functions as a metonymy that represents speech. But the description of the tongue is more than literary language. The tongue is a physical part of the body, and it represents a connection to both what is outside the body and to what comes from within the body. On the one hand, the tongue is influenced by other realms and powers external to itself, and on the other hand, it represents the thoughts and intentions of the inner person. Speech can be used to encourage, to lift others up, to compliment, and ultimately to bless. Blessing takes place as we look into the eyes of another person often accompanied by gentle appropriate touch and speak their true identity: child of God, beloved, worthy, honored. But speech is also used to abuse others: hate speech that tears people down based on their religion, race, or sexuality. Many think they are justified in speaking of people who are not like themselves as if they deserve hatred and disrespect. James describes the tongue as "a restless evil, full of deadly poison." There are literally ways in which humans can kill each other with their speech. Unfortunately, there have been more and more instances of young people killing themselves after experiencing hateful and bullying speech and images posted about them on social media.[135] Others may think that their speech doesn't cross a line because it hasn't played to racist ideas or prejudicial thinking while at the same time using their words to build themselves up at the expense of others. For many, the easiest people to harm with one's tongue are those with whom we are the most familiar: family and friends. The very intimacy of our relationships gives us knowledge that we can use to deeply wound our closest relationships with words. A short meditation on how we have used our own speech either for our own advantage or to wound others in anger as well as contemplating how we have been wounded by the speech of others should make us keenly aware of the challenges James points to in this passage.

135. Bottaro 2023.

At the same time, this passage does not present a strategy for controlling the tongue. There is no instruction to be silent or to refrain from speech (although earlier in the book James did encourage his audience to be "slow to speak" [1:19]). Instead, James simply indicates that the double-standard of speaking well of God while harming others with one's tongue shouldn't be. The implication of the natural metaphors is that we are to be single-minded, people of faith, and trust in God, growing in actions and deeds that reflect that single-minded trust as well as growing in speech and words that reflect our reception of the implanted word, lodged deeply in both the inner self and the Christian community.

Commentary

THE WISDOM FROM ABOVE (JAMES 3:13–18)

James 3:13–18: Who is wise and understanding among you? By his good conduct let him demonstrate his works with humble wisdom. (14) But if you have bitter envy and selfish ambition in your hearts, do not boast and lie against the truth. (15) This is not the wisdom coming down from above but it is earthly, natural, demonic. (16) For where there is envy and selfish ambition, there is disorder and every kind of evil deed. (17) But the wisdom from above is first pure, then peaceable, gentle, willing to yield, full of mercy and good fruits, without judgment, unfeigned. (18) And the fruit of righteousness is sown in peace by those who make peace.

James once again begins a section with a question (cf. 2:14). And just as 3:1 begins by warning that not many *among you* should desire to be teachers, so too this question asks who *among you* is wise and understanding. Some scholars continue to see this as a passage addressed to teachers,[136] but wisdom and understanding are not reserved for the teachers in the congregation. This section should be seen as continuing to address the whole congregation—all those who have received the implanted word are to conduct themselves in ways that are congruent with that word. James switches from the vocabulary of "tongue" to the topic of "wisdom." Yet even in the midst of introducing a new topic, Jas 3:13–18 draws on many themes and ideas that have already been explored in earlier parts of James. The idea of instability or restlessness (1:8; 3:8, 16). Other links refer us back to wisdom (1:5), righteousness (1:20; 2:23), humility or meekness (1:21), and things that come from above (1:17). Similarly, the word "bitter" (3:11) also shows up in this passage. The contrast that is so evident in this passage is between a wise life that is exemplified with humble action and the life characterized by bitter envy and selfish ambition. Ultimately, the person whose life is characterized by the wisdom that comes from above becomes one who sows and makes peace. While there is no direct connection between the topics of teachers and the tongue in 3:1–12 and the topic of wisdom in 3:13–18, one can also notice that teachers who exhibit wisdom and the tongue that shares the characteristics of 3:17–18 will be more in line with godly wisdom from above than with the powers of hell in 3:6.

The whole congregation ("who among you") is invited to consider who in their midst is wise and understanding. "The adjective *sophos* can be used . . . as a substantive for a 'wise person' in the sense of being practically

---

136. McKnight 2011: 302.

skilled... or generally learned.... It was the designation applied to the legendary sages of Greece... and Israel."[137] While we might associate wisdom with head knowledge, to be a sage was to be a person whose wisdom was worthy of imitation, and in the ancient world people often learned by associating themselves with a wise person—becoming that person's disciples. In other words, the connection between learning, understanding, and wisdom is not solely head knowledge but rather wisdom gained through life together, through imitation, and through practice. James explicitly identifies the wise as those who have good conduct or behavior and do good deeds. As Johnson notes, their behavior or conduct "denotes an entire manner of life."[138] These good deeds are ones that are performed with humble wisdom. Both Jews and early Christians valued humility as a virtuous part of moral behavior even though Greeks and Romans "associated it with meanness and groveling."[139] Humility is associated with gentleness, mildness, and considerateness. Deeds done with wisdom characterized by humility are the opposite of deeds done for self-promotion or with the ambition of impressing others or gaining self-importance.

James 3:14 contrasts the wisdom of verse 13 that is demonstrated through a life of humble good works with lives characterized by bitter envy and selfish ambition. Once again, James reminds his reader of their choice between two ways: in this case, the way of humble wisdom or the way of envy and selfish ambition. This second way is one filled with intensely negative feelings about the success of other people and one's own lack of such success. Before New Testament times this word for selfish ambition (*eritheia*) is only found in Aristotle, where it refers to someone who seeks political office for themselves and uses unfair means to obtain that office.[140] Out of this idea, the word comes to refer to selfish ambition, to a life that is far more concerned with one's own status and position than the well-being of others or of one's community. Here, we should recognize that good deeds can be done for the purpose of self-promotion and in order to look good in the eyes of others. This is why it is so crucial for James that the life that reflects wisdom consists of good deeds done with humble wisdom. It takes a certain kind of person, a person shaped by the virtues that are listed in verse 17, to see the needs of others, to have the wisdom to meet those

---

137. Johnson 1995: 270.
138. Johnson 1995: 270.
139. Laws 1993: 160.
140. BDAG, 392.

needs, and the humility not to boast about those deeds. Those whose lives are characterized by envy and selfish ambition will boast about their deeds (good or bad), lie about their accomplishments, and in this way undermine the truth. The word "truth" is only used two other times in James. It first occurs in Jas 1:18 where the readers are reminded that God has given birth to them "by the word of truth." Then, the readers are invited to receive "the implanted word that is able to save" their lives. If the readers boast about their envy, about their ambition, about their deeds, they are giving the lie to the word of truth that was the instrument of their salvation. The word "truth" happens one more time in Jas 5:19, which describes someone who wanders from the truth. Such wandering is not just moving away from objective truth. It is wandering away from God, the creator who gave birth to his people by the word of truth, both spoken in creation and incarnated in Jesus Christ.

This type of so-called wisdom does not come down from above (v. 15). James has already told us what comes from above—every good and perfect gift. The unchanging father of lights, the creator of the universe, gives gifts, especially the gift of his truthful word (1:17–18). To speak and act in ways that abuse or ignore or deny the gifts of God and the power of his truthful word to save is to act in ways that are at complete odds with God. James describes this way of acting and this so-called wisdom as "earthly, natural, and demonic." This is the opposite of that which is spiritual and godly. Those whose lives are characterized by selfish ambition are aligned with the forces of evil, those demonic forces that put their own interests and ambitions ahead of their heavenly creator. Martha Moore-Keish notes that some might think that James's identification of this way of living as "earthly" could be seen as a rejection of the goodness of the material world—of bodies and of creation itself.[141] However, as she notes, to read the text this way is to deny the importance that Judaism and early Christianity placed on the goodness of the body (one of the reasons bodily resurrection is such an important Christian doctrine). Indeed, James does not go on to imagine a disembodied "spiritual" life but rather depicts an embodied life of purity, peacefulness, and gentleness that has fruitful results. Instead, once again James's readers are asked to choose: will they live a life associated with envy and selfish ambition or will they choose a life associated with God's wisdom? In verse 16, James draws out the conclusion that where envy and selfish ambition are present so too are instability and every evil

---

141. Moore-Keish 2019: 133–34.

deed. Here, James uses the noun "instability" (*akatastasia*), which is related to the adjective "unstable" (*akatastatos*) found in the unstable person of 1:8 and the untamed restless tongue of 3:8. Both individuals and communities whose aims are envious and selfish end up generating turmoil that causes disorder. And not just disorder but "every evil deed." Adamson reminds us that evil actions were a part of the early church. And it would be naïve to think that those whose orientation is driven by envy and ambition would not resort to evil actions to accomplish their purposes, even within the sacred boundaries of the church.

Verse 17 now establishes the contrast drawn out by wisdom from above. Such wisdom is first pure or holy. While James does not use this word elsewhere, his focus on religion that is clean and unstained in 1:27 foreshadows the placement of "purity" in this list of virtues that characterize the wise. Here, purity serves as the "heading for what follows: those who are truly 'pure' or 'holy' will in fact be peaceable, gentle, and so on."[142] The quality of being a peace-loving person takes first place in the enumerated list and is further emphasized by the repetition of "peace" in the saying found in verse 18. This quality is in direct contrast to the "wars" and "arguments" that characterize the beginning of James 4. The peace-loving person is also characterized by gentleness. This is not a person who insists on their rights (in other words, it is the opposite of selfish ambition which is always attending to what is rightfully my own and how I might gain more) but rather yields to others with kindness and tolerance. The next word, *eupeithēs*, only occurs here in the whole Bible. Various translations have been offered, including: "open to reason" (ESV, RSV, sim. NASB), "accommodating" (NET), "submissive" (NIV, note that this is not the same word that is translated as "submissive" or "submit" elsewhere in the NT), and "willing to yield" (NRSV, NLT). Dibelius clarifies the meaning of this word as follows: "He who heeds one who is giving proper advice, and follows willingly such a one is tractable."[143] In other words, a person who is led and taught easily. He goes on to note that this characteristic, along with deference and kindly speech, were to characterize the relationship between brothers in the ancient world. The person who is filled with the wisdom from above is also described as being full of mercy and good fruits. To have mercy is to show compassion towards another person. This is a well-known attribute of God. The translators of the Septuaigint often translated

142. Allison 2013: 581.
143. Dibelius 1975: 214.

references to God's steadfast love (*hesed*) with the Greek word *eleos*, "mercy." Those who demonstrate wisdom from above are filled with compassion for others. As is true throughout James so far, the demonstration of alignment with God and God's purposes is best seen by how one acts and what one chooses to do. This continues to be true in this list characterizing wisdom. Good fruit—in other words, good deeds—are the outcome of wisdom. Finally, the last two characteristics of our list are "unwavering" and "sincere." In contrast to the instability caused by earthly wisdom (v. 16, *akatastasia*), the wisdom that comes from God is not divisive but steady. It is sincere or unfeigned (the opposite of hypocritical). This is the genuine authenticity that people long to find among Christians. These people are not trying to look better than they are, flatter others, or gain their own position but rather are genuinely sincere in their words and actions.

As he has done in other sections (Jas 2:13, 26), James wraps up this paragraph about who is wise with a short pithy saying. Like similar sayings, this one has a certain ambiguity that invites the reader to ponder it, turn it over in the mind, and wrestle with its meaning. The imagery here is striking. A group of people who are referred to as "peacemakers" are sowing. The thing that is being sown is "the fruit of righteousness." Fruit refers to the part of the plant that contains seeds that will themselves grow to produce new plants and new fruit. In other words, this reproductive metaphor points to the generative reality of peace making. The fruit consists of righteousness. "For James and his Jewish world of thought, 'righteous' described the person whose behaviors and life were in conformity with Torah. What James has in mind in this metaphorical expression is the yield of acting rightly, namely, concrete acts of justice."[144] The way the fruit of righteousness is being sown is "in peace." Peace refers to harmony between people. This saying comes immediately before a set of questions about the causes of community conflict. In contrast to such conflict, justice and good deeds come about in the context of harmonious relationships among God's people. But peaceful relationships don't just happen. Rather, there are people who are noted for their ability to make peace. This reminds us of the saying of Jesus, "Blessed are the peacemakers, for they will be called children of God" (Matt 5:9). In a world full of war, conflict, and dispute, God's people are called to be those who make peace (not just keeping the peace or being peaceable people). Making peace can be costly. Instead of rivalry, self-serving ambition, and boasting, being a peace maker means bringing

144. McKnight 2011: 319.

together people who are divided with the goal of creating harmony across a variety of barriers. Those who practice making peace are deeply engaged in the work of loving their neighbor and bringing about justice in the world.

Fusing the Horizons

One temptation is to associate wisdom and understanding with speech and knowledge. But James does not do this. Instead, he indicates that wisdom is demonstrated by one's life. A life of good conduct and humble deeds is the true demonstration of wisdom. We might even go further and say that the life of deeds teaches as much as or more than the life of words. In the ancient world teaching involved not only the accumulation of knowledge but the invitation to observe the life of the teacher, to be the disciple of a teacher. The student learns by not only hearing what the teacher says but by watching the teacher's actions. Whose life among our local congregations stands out to us as worthy of being emulated? Not because the person is wealthy or sophisticated or clever but because that person has the wisdom to see what is needed and to act with humility in ways that meet that need. Such a person acts with no intention for self-promotion but instead out of a pure heart of integrity with care, mercy, and kindness. These are the people we are invited to see as the wise ones among us. And when the community faces conflict, the peacemakers who are living lives of peace, gentleness, and good deeds are those we should seek to help restore peace in the community.

Friend of the World or Enemy of God? (James 4:1–12)

James 4:1–12 Where do the wars and quarrels among you come from? Do they not come from this, from your desires which wage war among your members? (2) You desire and you do not possess, so you murder. And you are filled with jealous envy and you are not able to obtain, so you quarrel and wage war. You do not have because you do not ask; (3) you ask and do not receive because you ask wickedly, in order that you may indulge your pleasures. (4) You adulteresses! Do you not know that friendship with the world is hostility towards God? Therefore, whoever wants to be a friend of the world, that one makes himself an enemy of God. (5) Or do you think that the scripture speaks vainly? The spirit which he caused to dwell in us longs enviously, (6) but he gives greater grace. Therefore it says: "God opposes the proud, but gives grace to the humble." (7) Therefore humble yourselves before God, resist the devil and he will flee from you; draw near to God and he will draw near to you. Cleanse your hands, you sinners, and purify your hearts, you double-minded. Be miserable and mourn and weep. Let your laughter be turned into mourning and your joy into gloom. (10) Humble yourselves before the Lord and he will lift you up. (11) Do not speak evil against one another, brothers and sisters. The one who speaks evil against his brother or sister or who judges his brother or sister speaks evil against the law and judges the law; but if you judge the law, you are not a doer of the law but a judge. (12) There is one lawgiver and judge, the one able to save and to destroy. But you, who are you to judge your neighbor?

Here, James turns from the wisdom and peaceable living of 3:13–18 to the strife that is disrupting the lives of his audience. Once again James spells out that misdirected desire and allegiances to things that are contrary to God leads to conflict, lack, and distance from God. But at the end of the passage, there is a clear path to restoration of relationship between God and humanity and a restoration of relationship between humans. This passage can be outlined like this: Jas 4:1–3 lays out the problem: dangerous speech that leads to conflict in the church. James 4:4–6 lays out what they should already know, namely that they can either choose the way of God, which is the way of humility, or the way of the world, which is the way of the jealous spirit that inhabits humans. James 4:7–10 shows how to restore right relationship with God through humility and repentance. Finally, Jas 4:11–12 lays out the solution to the problem in 4:1–3, namely instead of quarreling and operating out of selfish motives, don't slander other brothers and sisters. Maintain humility by recognizing that only God is the true lawgiver and judge. This outline sees Jas 4:11–12 as an integral part of the wisdom instruction James is laying out for the church.

James 4:1 begins this section with two questions. First, where do the wars and quarrels among you come from? He then answers his question with a second question, don't these come from your desires which wage war among your members? The Greek (*ouk*) indicates that this second question should be answered yes. Yes, this conflict does indeed come from your misplaced or inordinate desires. This verse is saturated with the language of war, conflict, and argument. It is the exact opposite of the peacemaking that is described in 3:18. Everyone who lived in the Roman Empire lived in a military dictatorship where peace was obtained through the deployment of military legions at the borders and the exercise of governmental power throughout the provinces. War and conflict were ever present realities. But this was not to be the reality of the church. James, like Jesus before him, has just pointed the church toward peacemaking. This portion of James is filled with words that connote desire, usually in a negative sense. In 4:1, *hēdonē*, from which we get our word hedonism, describes the desire that fuels conflict. "In the NT ἡδονή [*hēdonē*] represents one of the many forces which belong to the world of unsanctified carnality, which strive against the work of God and His Spirit, and which drag [humans] back again into the kingdom of evil."[145] This conflict takes place "among your members." This phrase can be understood in two different ways. One way is to understand that individuals within the group experience illicit pleasures or desires and that those individuals conduct their own internal battle against those desires. The other way to understand the end of this section is to see the war that unfolds as one that happens among the members of the church. The desires fueled by the systems of this world bring about conflict within the church.

James goes on to indicate that they have a longing or a desire that they are not able to bring to fulfillment, so they participate in murder. Craig Keener notes that hyperbole is part of the genre of this section and is used for rhetorical effect. In the previous unit (3:13–18), he noted the possibility that some among the Christians might have advocated for "zeal" to overthrow those they opposed. He continues, "Most of James's readers have presumably not literally killed anyone, but they are exposed to violent teachers (3:13–18) who regard murder as a satisfactory means of attaining justice

---

145. *TDNT*, 2:910.

Commentary

and redistribution of wealth."[146] In contrast to those who might advocate for conflict, James advocates for prayer. Their unfulfilled desire drives them to conflict and war among themselves. Those who participate in this conflict are serving themselves rather than aiming for peace that flows from the wisdom of God. James then tells them that they don't have because they don't ask. In other words, their prayer life is lacking. The sentence continues in verse 3 with the assertion that when they do ask, they don't receive because they ask wickedly. The evil intention connected to their asking is that they are not asking for the benefit of the community but rather to fulfill their intention to spend freely on their pleasures. James once again uses the word *hēdonē*, pleasure, to describe desires that are driven by alignment with the forces of this world rather than with God. Not all pleasure is wrong. Indeed, God himself is the creator of beauty and abundance, but trying to use prayer for gain that is then spent on those things that are not part of God's way is an example of abusing the gift of prayer. In Jas 1:5, those who lack wisdom are invited to ask for it with faith from the God who gives. In other words, the focus of prayer in James 1 is on receiving wisdom and being a person who is able to trust that God is one who will hear and respond to that prayer. In contrast, in James 4 the person who is embedded in conflict is (1) not asking at all (one wonders if this is because they don't think they need to—they have a certain arrogance that points to self-sufficiency). Or (2) when they do ask, they don't receive because they ask with wicked motives for things that are not right to ask for. James 1 indicates one of the good things to ask for—wisdom. In contrast, this is an example of people who ask for something in order to satisfy themselves by spending it on their own pleasures.

After this indictment of the conflict among them, their misplaced desires, and the impact it has on their prayer life, James harshly calls out his audience as Adulteresses! The term is not speaking specifically about women here but rather is a harsh judgment of the audience's lack of faithfulness to the ways of God. In some ways this is reminiscent of the Old Testament prophets. Hosea provides one example, "Hear the word of the LORD, O people of Israel; for the LORD has an indictment against the inhabitants of the land. There is no faithfulness or loyalty, and no knowledge of God in the land. Swearing, lying, and murder, and stealing and adultery break out; bloodshed follows bloodshed" (Hos 4:1–2). Once again, James asks his audience a question and expects them to answer yes. They do know

---

146. Keener 2014: 679.

that to have friendship with the world is to place themselves in the position of being enemies of God. In many ways, this is the climax of the two-ways theology of James. Someone can choose God's way of living in the world, or someone can choose the world's system of life. "Those who claimed to be God's friends (Jas 2:23) but were really moral clients of the world (friendship often applied to patron-client relationships)—that is, they shared the world's values (3:13–18)—were really unfaithful to God"[147] Friendship was an important value in the ancient world. Alicia Batten writes, "We have seen that qualities such as loyalty, faithfulness, being of 'one mind/one soul,' sharing possessions, as well as proving one's friendship through trials, were commonly associated with friendship, appearing in Graeco-Roman, Jewish and Christian sources."[148] The question for James is whether one intends to share these attributes of friendship with God or with the world. There is no neutral position where the person can stand apart; rather, there is either relationship with God or relationship with the world. The final part of Jas 4:4 returns us to the question, "What do you want?" There is desire for God or desire for the world, but these two desires are incompatible. Choose one or choose the other. The one who wants to be a friend of the world makes himself an enemy of God. To be an enemy is to be characterized by hate and hostility towards God. This attitude towards God is one that the person who makes himself an enemy of God chooses.

In Jas 4:5 we arrive at one of the most challenging New Testament verses. This verse presents two kinds of problems. The first problem is that the beginning of the verse appears to introduce a quotation; however, there isn't anything in the Old Testament or in extra-biblical literature that matches the remainder of verse 5. There are several solutions that have been proposed for this problem. The first solution is to acknowledge that James is using a quotation but that it is from a source we no longer have access to. The second solution is to suggest that James's "quotation" is actually a summary of several verses and ideas from the Old Testament. The third solution is to suggest that what follows the introductory formula "the Scripture says" is a parenthetical comment and that the actual Scripture citation begins in verse 6. In this case, the words "therefore it says" would be a resumption of the phrase "the Scripture says" in verse 5 with the quotation now following. Since there is no known source for the words in the second half of verse 5, it seems better to me to see the words in verse 5 as a parenthetical comment.

147. Keener 2014: 679.
148. Batten 2010: 55.

Commentary

The second problem in verse 5 relates to both the meaning and function of the words that make up the second half of the verse. This problem impacts the way we understand the verse. In order to demonstrate some of the issues in this verse, the chart below uses underlining to point out variations in English translations that impact the meaning of the verse. All the translations agree that this is a question that begins along the lines, "Do you think that the scripture speaks vainly . . ." The significant differences follow:

he jealously longs for the <u>spirit</u> he has caused to dwell in us? (NIV)

"He yearns jealously over the <u>spirit</u> that he has made to dwell in us"? (ESV)

the <u>Spirit</u> He caused to dwell in us yearns with envy? (Berean Standard Bible)

The <u>spirit</u> that dwelleth in us lusteth to envy? (KJV)

"He jealously desires the <u>Spirit</u> whom He has made to dwell in us"? (NASB)

"The <u>spirit</u> that God caused to live within us has an envious yearning"? (NET)

First, note that three of our translations (ESV, NASB, NET) take this as a quotation, while the other three do not. The first set reflects that the second half of the verse is introduced by a classic quotation formula ("the scripture says"), while the second set reflects the fact that there is no known verse in Scripture that corresponds to this portion of Jas 4:5.

Second, note that the word *pneuma* is capitalized in some translations (BSB, NASB) reflecting the position that the word refers to the Holy Spirit, while other translations do not capitalize the word and see it as referring to the human spirit.

Third, note that the word *phthonos* is sometimes translated as "jealousy" (NIV, ESV, NASB), which can be understood positively or negatively. Other translations use the English word "envy," which has a negative meaning. In biblical literature *phthonos* is always used negatively and does *not* have the sense of "zeal." Zeal is the positive meaning of the more common Greek word *zēlos*, which has both the positive meaning "zeal" and the negative meaning "jealousy" or "envy." The word used here, *phthonos*, is not used anywhere else to refer to God's righteous jealousy. Instead, it is always used negatively, to refer to envy or jealousy in a negative sense. In this verse it is best to retain the sense of "envy" and to understand that this is not an emotion that is characteristic of either God or the Holy Spirit.

Finally, note that the KJV reads "the spirit that dwells" while the rest of the translations read "caused to dwell." The KJV is based on Greek manuscripts that were available in the early 1600s as well as previous English translations, such as those made by Tyndale and Coverdale. Since that time many additional Greek manuscripts have been made available to scholars. Some of these are very ancient (dating to the 400s and sometimes earlier) and are of superior quality to the manuscripts that were known in the 1600s. These more ancient manuscripts have a slightly different verb that means "caused to dwell," and most modern translations understand that this is the reading that is appropriate for this verse.

These observations lead me to interpret the verse along the lines of the NET: "The [human] spirit that God caused to live within us has an envious yearning." However, I do not see this as a quotation from an unknown source but rather as a parenthetical comment. This points to two ideas. First, the human spirit is one that has been created by God. Since this is the case, the expectation may be that the one who is created by God should long for the things of God. But the rest of this saying points to the second idea. The reality is that the human spirit is one that is full of envy. This statement is not surprising in the midst of a unit that has raised questions about the conflicts they experience, has indicated that these conflicts originate in misplaced desire, and has pointed to covetousness in the community. These things are part of "friendship with the world." Such a way of life is directly opposed to the wisdom from above (3:13–18) that is characterized by holiness, peacefulness, gentleness, and the other virtues of verse 17.

Translators and Translations: As a Christian, it can be troubling to read about the uncertainty behind the translation of particular verses, especially in cases like Jas 4:5 where there are quite a few options related to how the verse can be translated. Skilled scholars who have spent many years studying Greek can have disagreements about the best way to translate a particular verse or phrase. Sometimes these disagreements are minor and don't have a significant impact on our understanding of the verse in English. But in some cases, such as this one, there really are significant differences. It is quite different to say that the human spirit is envious than to say that the Holy Spirit is jealous. It is also different to say that the human spirit that God caused to dwell in us is envious—with

Commentary

perhaps a sense that the human spirit that God made shouldn't be like that—than it is to say that the spirit dwelling in us is envious. Where do such differences come from? And what are Christians to think about these differences in biblical translation?

Differences in translation can arise from two basic sources. First, there can be ambiguity in the construction of the Greek sentence itself. We recognize this in English. For example, the sentence: "I watched the dog run away with my glasses" could either mean that the dog ran away with the glasses or it could mean that I was wearing glasses and saw the dog run away. The ambiguity is part of the grammar of the sentence. The same thing can happen in Greek. Second, there are many, many manuscripts of the Greek New Testament. By some estimates there are over five thousand manuscripts of the Greek New Testament. Some of these are just fragments while others contain large portions of the New Testament. Over time, as scribes hand copied the text, errors can be introduced into the Greek text. Both sentence ambiguity and variations in the Greek text contribute to the differences in our English translations.

Here, it is helpful to know that most modern Bible translations are produced by committees of scholars who work together to create a translation that is as accurate as possible. When there are ambiguities in the text, scholars use a wide variety of tools to help resolve the issue. This includes attention to the meaning of the words that are being used (like the word *phthonos* in our verse), attention to the context in which the verse is found (here, the context seems to be negative and the reference to the human spirit rather than the Holy Spirit more appropriate—although translations are divided), attention to agreed upon principles for determining the most likely Greek words in the text (in our verse, this means the reading "caused to dwell" is preferred), and attention to the overall meaning of the verse and whether it corresponds to the rest of Scripture.

It's important to know that even when there is ambiguity, it is not so great as to challenge the facts and doctrines on which the Christian faith relies—the life, death, resurrection, and ascension of Jesus and the good news that through his death and resurrection all the peoples of the world are invited to receive salvation and become part of the household of God.

At the end of verse 5, it would be tempting to despair. After all, the community is teeming with conflict and jealousy that leaves them embedded in the values of the world. Yet, verse 6 begins with the hopeful word "but." "But greater grace he gives." In Greek, the word "greater" is brought

James

to the front of the sentence where it emphasizes the quantity and quality of the grace that is offered by God in comparison to the reality of the envious human spirit that drives the conflict of the earlier verses. The reader is reminded once again of God's character. He is the God who gives (Jas 1:5) good and perfect gifts (1:17). Here, the gift that God gives is "grace." The word "grace" (*charis*) in Greek literally means gift. God as the patron of the Christian community gives first and foremost the gift of himself along with all other good and perfect gifts. While God gives generously to all, such gifts also create obligation on the part of the receiver.[149]

And now, the text turns to a quotation from scripture to support the assertion that God gives greater grace. The quotation comes from Prov 3:34, a verse that comes near the end of a section that shares themes with James. Proverbs 3:27–28, "Do not withhold to do good to the needy, when your hand can help. Do not say, 'Go, come back, and tomorrow, I will give,' when you are able to do good, for you do not know what the next day will bring" (NETS). James 2:14–16 with its comment on those who send people away with words of peace without providing for their needs resembles this instruction. Similarly, Prov 3:30, "Do not quarrel with anyone without a cause, lest he does some harm to you" (NETS), shares a theme against quarreling and conflict found in Jas 4:1–3. At the end of this passage from Proverbs about caring for those in need, about not quarreling, and about pursuing righteousness (Prov 3:31–33), the text of James quoting Proverbs says, "God opposes the proud, but gives grace to the humble." The proud are those whose lives are characterized by jealousy, quarreling, and selfish ambition. They are concerned with their own status over care for others. In contrast, it is the humble who are recipients of God's grace. These are the people whose faith is characterized by works of mercy directed to the poor, people who are characterized by peace rather than quarreling, and people who seek to live in right relationship with God and others. Notice that God's grace is not given to "all" but rather to the humble in contrast to the proud. In the verses that follow, James will demonstrate how one who is not already humble might move towards humility.

James 4:7–10 makes heavy use of the imperative verb, the language of command, followed by the future tense. The sense is, "Do this, and then this will happen." The first command is to submit to God. This is the overarching instruction that governs this whole portion of the text. It is bookended in verse 10 with the command to humble yourself before the Lord. In other

---

149. See excursus on Gifts in the First Century and Today.

words, the whole unit is surrounded by the concept of submitting or humbling. And we have just seen that it is this very group, the humble, to whom God gives the gift of his divine favor and attention (4:6).

In between the opening and closing verses, James provides eight ways to practice submission and humility. It begins with resisting the devil. We have already seen that wisdom that is opposed to God, that resists God, is "devilish" (3:15) and that choosing friendship with the world is to choose opposition to God, to choose a position as "enemy of God" (4:4). If one wishes to submit to God, then one must resist the devil—the power behind the systems of this world that stands in opposition to God. In 4:6 the same verb is used of God resisting or opposing the proud. Now, those who are aligned with the humble are instructed to resist the devil and his temptations. The promise is that the devil will flee from those who resist him. Verse 8 continues the sentence by instructing the reader to draw near to God and promises that the outcome will be that God will draw near to them. Once again, the text presents the reader with a choice. With whom are they allied? The answer to that question is found by awareness of what or who one is resisting and what or who one is drawing near to. Will the readers choose the devil and the systems of this world that are influenced by deception, selfish ambition, and other vices? Those who do not oppose him are by definition drawing closer to him. Those who resist will find that his power fades away as he flees. Will the readers choose God? Those who do not choose God, who do not draw near to them, are by James's definition opposing God. There is no neutral position—there is only the choice between the God who gives or the devil and the powers behind this world.

Luke Timothy Johnson notes that "in the symbolic world of Torah, the notion of 'approaching God' inevitably has ritual overtones. . . . God dwells in a realm of purity. Approaching God demands self-purification."[150] The call is to purify both hands and heart. The picture is of moral purity in both action and intent. But while the call is to purity, the audience is addressed as "sinners" and "double-minded" (cf. 1:8). In Jas 4:4, the text referred to the readers as "adulteresses," now it calls them "sinners." Those who should have been faithful have become unfaithful. They have cheated on God by giving their allegiance to other gods and other ways of living in the world. Those who should have been obedient to God's covenant commands, including the commands to care for the poor and to be people of integrity, have failed to keep covenant with God thus being marked as sinners. The

150. Johnson 1995: 285.

image of washing the hands connects to purification associated with priests and the day of atonement (Lev 16:4, 30), but it also is an image of moral purity. So, the Psalmist asks, "Who shall ascend the hill of the LORD? And who shall stand in his holy place? Those who have cleans hands and pure hearts, who do not lift up their souls to what is false, and do not swear deceitfully" (Ps 24:3–4). Similarly, "James's focus is on the heart's wayward nature: it can be deceived (1.26); it can be the source of communal strife (3.14); it can be impure and so in need of cleansing (4.8); and it can luxuriate in pleasure while others suffer (5.5)."[151] To cleanse the hands is to seek purity in action. To purify the heart is to be single-minded in intention, oriented towards faithfulness, in contrast to the double-minded, who try to choose two ways at the same time.

Verse 9 follows with a trio of three related commands: lament, mourn, and weep. These are the responses of those who have been caught in selfish conflict, adultery, disobedience, and double mindedness. In Psalm 38,[152] David laments over his sin with phrases like "there is no peace for my bones" (v. 3), "my acts of lawlessness . . . like a heavy burden they weighed on me" (v. 4), and "my wounds stank and festered" (v. 5). This is the context in which Ps 38:6 (LXX Ps 37:7) makes use of the same Greek word found in James: "I was wretched" (NETS). The word means to be miserable or to endure distress or sorrow. This can be expressed as lament, but it is more than just words. It is the embodied feeling that leads one to cry out, "O Lord, before you is all my desire, and my groaning was not hidden from you" (Ps 38:9; LXX 37:10 NETS). Towards the end of the Psalm, David confesses his sin (v. 18, LXX v. 19) and calls on the Lord to help him (v. 22, LXX v. 23). The second command in this trio is "mourn." This is the common word that is used to describe the sadness and grief that accompanies death or disaster and is the opposite of joy.[153] Mourning is also found in prophetic texts such as Amos, which point out the failure of the people of Israel to care for the poor and then proclaims the Lord's coming judgment, a judgment that will result in mourning for the people of the land (Amos 8:8).[154] God's judgment is the rightful naming of the way things are in the

---

151. Allison 2013: 573.

152. LXX Ps 37 with different verse numbers. The translation is from NETS but references are to standard English texts of the Psalms.

153. BDAG, 795.

154. Other examples of God's judgment leading to mourning can be found in Isa 3:16–26; Jer 14:1–11. In the NT, 1 Cor 5:2 records Paul's frustration with the Corinthians who should have mourned about sin rather than being arrogant and prideful about the

Commentary

world and among God's people. When God's people have done wrong, God names that wrong. Ultimately, those who can hear God's just judgment of their wrongdoing are then afforded the opportunity to repent, which can then lead to their restoration. Those who cannot hear the right naming of their sin cannot mourn their failure, and they begin to turn towards God and the right way of living. Lament and mourning lead to tears, to weeping or crying over sin. The second half of the verse continues the themes of the first half. Laughter is to be turned to mourning and joy into dejection. Both of these instructions involve reversal. The movement from laughter and joy to sadness. In Jas 1:2, joy was the lens through which to understand trials, but here there is nothing to be joyful about. Instead, repentance involves the recognition of wrongdoing and desolation over the sin itself and its consequences.

James 4:7–10 wraps up with a return to humility, an echo of the submission found in the opening instruction of Jas 4:7. The audience is instructed to humble itself before the Lord and promised that he will lift them up. This reversal is one that is in the Lord's hands rather than their own. In contrast to the self-promotion that is characterized by selfish ambition (3:14), quarrels (4:1), jealousy (4:2), and prayer directed towards the fulfillment of one's own wicked pleasures (4:3), those who wish to draw near to God take on the posture of humility. Any exaltation that takes place is brought about by God in God's time. Any increase in honor or position or power will come from God. Even those who are exalted by God must maintain a position of submission to and humility before God. Those who fail to do so will once again find themselves embroiled in selfish ambition, quarreling, and misplaced motives; they will find themselves once more aligning themselves as friends of the world rather than friends of God.

After having referred to the audience as "adulteresses, sinners, and double-minded," James now addresses them once again as "brothers and sisters." In this way, he reminds them of their identity not as warring factions but as kin, as those committed to working together for the good of the whole community. As such, slanderous words and unjust judgments have no place in the community. The words of Jas 4:11 are reminiscent of the saying of Jesus recorded in Matt 7:1, "Do not judge in order that you may not be judged." Both Jesus and James draw on the law of love and its relationship to speech in Lev 19:15–18: "You shall not render an unjust judgment; you shall not be partial to the poor or defer to the great; with

---

sin in their midst.

justice you shall judge your neighbor. You shall not go around as a slanderer among your people.... You shall not hate in your heart anyone of your kin.... You shall not take vengeance or bear a grudge against any of your people, but you shall love your neighbor as yourself: I am the LORD." In James, the law has been summed up as "loving one's neighbor as oneself" (Jas 2:8). Those who slander ("speak evil about") their brothers and sisters are not living according to the law of love that James has already spelled out. In fact, in contrast to the attitude of submission and humility that characterizes Jas 4:7-10, those who slander their brothers and sisters are exalting themselves at the expense of others. James uses "slander" and "judge" as virtual synonyms. "For one human being to slander another means that the status of a *judge* has been assumed. The other is measured, found wanting, and is condemned—all in secret."[155] Those who slander and so judge their brother or sister, speak against the law and judge the law. In other words, by their very thoughts and actions, they set themselves above the law and choose which laws apply to them and which do not. Indeed, those who judge their brothers and sisters have placed themselves in the position of God, who is the one true lawgiver and judge. Moreover, it is God alone who can save or destroy. James has already laid out for his audience God's role as the one who gave birth to them (1:18) and whose word is able to save (1:21). In contrast to the slanderous words of humans, God's word—God's law, God's judgment—this is what saves, but it is also God's word, God's just judgment, that destroys those who ultimately choose friendship with the world. On the closing question, Scot McKnight writes:

> One is tempted to translate the last question of this verse with "Who in the world do you think you are?" The "you," which is emphatic here, is defined: "you" is the one who judges, the one who stands over his neighbor in the way that God stands over all creation. Here James draws us into the Jesus Creed, the use of Deuteronomy 6:4-5 and Leviticus 19:18 as the foundational ethical directive for each follower of Jesus (Mark 12:28-32). Instead of standing next to the neighbor in love, the teachers had assumed the position of God and were over the neighbor. This, I am suggesting, is where James has driven the teachers: their zeal, ambition, cravings, desires, and yearnings toward envy have driven them up the ladder to the point where they are now assuming the prerogative of the one God who is Lawgiver and Judge. Such is their hubris; such is their idolatry.[156]

---

155. Johnson 1995: 294.
156. While McKnight takes this passage as applying to the teachers in the

Commentary

Fusing the Horizons

Loving one's neighbor as oneself is just as needed today as it was in James's day. This action towards others begins with submission to and humility before God. And it begins with resistance to the devil and the whole system of this world. The world, especially the culture of the western world, promotes endless attention to wanting/desiring. The very purpose of advertising is to create desire for what one does not have—both the product and the life or lifestyle that the ad depicts. And at the root of conflict is "the world," where "the ultimate argument is a fist. Or a boot. Or a gun. Or a bomb. Violence, force, power—that's what counts. People may smile and appear friendly and civilized; society may appear open and generous; but if you go against them, if you challenge cherished assumptions, there are ways of making you feel their displeasure."[157] Resisting the devil and the system of this world may involve turning off the TV, the talk shows, and the media feeds and choosing actions that confound the world. It also involves rejecting the world's solution to problems—violence—and choosing love. Such resistance to the systems of this world includes care for the poor and marginalized. It includes generosity in time and money and energy. Attention to these very things may be ways of drawing near to God. In other words, our acts of love and mercy based on faith draw us deeper into a cycle of action based on that same faith in the generous giving God. If the church truly wants to be a friend of God, it seems important to choose the same friends that God chooses, and in Jas 2:5 God clearly chooses the poor. As a church, it is crucial to find ways to be with, listen to, and walk alongside those who are poor, vulnerable, and marginalized. When churches live in this way, some of the divisive focus on politics, rhetoric, and the desire to get one's own way may fall to the wayside as the devil and the devil's worldly system are resisted. A focus on humble relationship with God and with those whom God has chosen can lead to renewed friendship with God and to resistance of the world's values.

---

congregation, his focus on the hubris of those who speak in ways that place themselves in the position of God is helpful. McKnight 2011: 367.

157. Wright 2011: 27.

Denouncing Boasting and the Rich and Encouraging Patient Endurance (James 4:13–5:12)

James 4:13–5:12: Come now, you who say, "Today or tomorrow we will go to this city and stay there a year and engage in business and make a profit." (14) You do not know what tomorrow will bring or what your life will be; for you are a vapor appearing for a short time and then vanishing. (15) Instead, you are to say, "If the Lord wills, we will live and do this or that." (16) But now you boast in your arrogance; all such boasting is evil. (17) So, the one who knows to do well and does not do it, to him it is sin.

James 5:1: Come now, you rich, weep and howl because of the miseries that are coming upon you. (2) Your wealth has decayed and your clothes have become moth eaten, (3) your gold and silver have become corroded and their rust will be a witness against you and will eat your flesh like fire. You stored up treasure in the last days. (4) Behold! The wage of the workers who mowed your fields, the wage that was fraudulently withheld, cries out against you, and the cries of the harvesters have entered into the ears of the Lord of Hosts. (5) You lived in luxury on the earth and you lived a life of self-indulgence, you fattened your heart in the day of slaughter, (6) you condemned, you murdered the righteous one; the one that did not resist you.

James 5:7: Be patient, therefore, brothers and sisters, until the coming of the Lord. Behold the farmer receives the precious fruit of the earth after waiting patiently for it, until it receives the early and late rains. (8) You also be patient, strengthen your hearts because the coming of the Lord has come near. (9) Do not complain, brothers and sisters, against one another, so that you may not be judged; behold, the judge stands before the door. (10) Take as an example, brothers and sisters, the suffering and the patience of the prophets who spoke in the name of the Lord. (11) Behold, we consider blessed those who endured; you have heard of the endurance of Job and you have seen the end of the Lord that the Lord is very compassionate and merciful. (12) But before all things, my brothers and sisters, do not swear neither by heaven nor by earth nor any other oath. But your yes is to be yes and your no is to be no, so that you may not fall under judgment.

There is general agreement among scholars that Jas 4:13–17; 5:1–6, 7–11 (or 12) are all paragraphs that address specific groups and topics. There is less agreement about how or whether they are connected to each other. In this commentary, I see 4:13–17 and 5:1–6 sharing a general tone of denunciation. First, wealthy merchants are denounced for their arrogant pride and boasting. Then the rich are denounced for their mistreatment of workers and misuse of wealth. Many scholars see a new section, once again addressed to the brothers and sisters of the congregation, beginning in 5:7. However, I see Jas 5:7-11 as the response to the problem presented in 5:1-6, so it is best understood within the larger context of the condemnation of the rich. For this reason, this commentary keeps these paragraphs together but treats each section separately in what follows. In James 4 and the opening paragraph of chapter 5, James returns to the theme of wealth and improper boasting first introduced in James 1:9-11. In the chapters in between, James has warned against mistreatment of the poor (2:1-4, 14-16), boasting (3:5, using a different Greek word), and arrogance (4:6). Now, James addresses arrogant merchants (4:13-17) and denounces corrupt landowners (5:1-6) before encouraging patient endurance (5:7-12).

Condemnation of Arrogant Merchants (James 4:13-17)

This section (and the next) begins with the phrase "come now." While this Greek phrase is not found in the LXX or elsewhere in the NT, it is reminiscent of Isa 1:18, "Come now, let us argue it out, says the Lord: though your sins are like scarlet, they shall be like snow." There, "come now" is used in the context of both confronting sin and promising forgiveness. Here, it draws the readers' attention. This section of James is not introduced like many units in James are with the familial address to brothers and sisters but rather with an abrupt address to "those who say." This raises the question of the relationship of this group to the Christian community. On the one hand, they may be numbered among "the rich," a group that James consistently depicts as arrogant and oppressive towards others. On the other hand, James offers a corrective to their approach to business. They should learn to take the Lord into consideration when making plans and to see the whole of their life through the lens of faith. "Come now, you who say" introduces a critique of this group of merchants. These business people indicate that their future plans include four things: (1) they will go to a city of their choosing; (2) they will stay there for a year; (3) they will engage in business; and (4) they will make a profit. In the very next verse James makes it clear that these future plans are plans that are made apart from God. Those who are making these plans have failed to consider that they do not know what tomorrow will bring. They have also failed to consider the fact that their life has the same transitory nature as "mist" or "vapor." The word *atmis* usually means "smoke" or "mist" in a literal sense. But in Hos 13:3 we see it used metaphorically. The prophet speaks of those who keep on sinning and who make idols for themselves. This is a group of people who think they control their own lives and make their own gods. The judgment they encounter is that "they shall be like the morning mist" (Hos 13:3). Hosea points to four things that disappear quickly—mist, dew, chaff, and smoke—and compares the disappearance of these fleeting things to the fate of those who keep on sinning. Similarly, in James, "mist" is used metaphorically to describe the reality of our human lives that appear and then disappear or are destroyed. This is reminiscent of the fate of the rich in Jas 1:10, where the wealthy are described as those who pass away like grass flowers. Those who make plans apart from God have failed to take into consideration the lack of control they have over their plans. In this way, they reveal themselves to be those who are arrogant and boastful, more aligned with the values of the world than with those of God.

Verse 15 presents James's solution to the problem. Instead of simply declaring what one intends to do (v. 13), one should acknowledge that one's very existence and all the plans that one might make are utterly dependent upon God. James is not presenting a formula for speech. In other words, this is not an indication that one should go ahead with making whatever plans one wants to and then anoint those plans with the words, "If God wills." Instead, this way of speaking continues the focus on humility that has been present from the beginning of the book (1:10; 3:17; 4:10). Humble living involves acknowledging the limits of human knowledge and capacity and recognizing the need for dependance upon God and attention to God's will. This is an ethic for the whole of life.

While verse 15 reflects how they should speak and live, verse 16 indicates what they are actually doing. They are boasting in their arrogance. In a very vivid example of the use of this word, 2 Macc 9:8 tells about the downfall of the Seleucid Emperor Antiochus, "Thus he who only a little while before had thought in his superhuman *arrogance* that he could command the waves of the sea . . . was brought down to earth and carried in a litter, making the power of God manifest to all" (emphasis added). This wealthy ruler had thought that he was able to do whatever he pleased, but what he discovered was that the details of his life were not within his own control. His boasting was an audacious disregard for the power of God over his life. Luke Timothy Johnson notes this about boasting:

> There is nothing subtle about the form of arrogance displayed in 4:13–17. James characterizes it as *alazoneia*, universally recognizable in the Greco-Roman world as the quality of the boaster, the braggart, the pretentious person. At the most obvious level, the traders are criticized for their arrogant assumption that they can depend on the future. But at a deeper level they share the outlook of "the world" expressed by envy: that having is the same as being and that "selling and getting a profit" is a way of securing their *own* future.[158]

Those who fail to practice humble dependence on God in their planning are boasting about their own ability to control the unfolding details of their life. Verse 16 goes on to state that "all such boasting is evil." Evil relates to the world, the flesh, and the devil—the systems that oppose God and that draw the merchant into relationship with the world and thus hostility towards God.

James ends this section with another aphorism: "To the one who knows to do good and does not do it, to him it is a sin." James first begins to talk about sin in 1:14–15. There sin born out of temptation leads to death. He goes on to indicate that showing favoritism is a sin because it goes against the royal law of loving one's neighbor. Here, the temptation is to make plans apart from God. Instead of living with humility before God, the focus is on investing, winning, and making a profit. In this context, James encourages them to do what they know is right. Doing right includes caring for the widow and orphan (1:27); not showing prejudice or favoritism (2:1); not ignoring the needs of the destitute (2:15–16); not misusing the tongue (3:9; 4:1); pursuing wisdom (1:5); and loving one's neighbor (2:8). The merchant who knows the right thing to do, the way to live in accordance with the law of love, is to live in that way.

Fusing the Horizons

James does not condemn merchants or business. What he condemns is the arrogant assumption that one's business plans are in some way separate from one's spiritual life and the assumption that a business person is able to control the outcome of their plans. The whole of one's life belongs to God including one's business, career, work, or resources. In our world today, it can be very tempting to live a divided life—a life of piety on Sundays and at

---

158. Johnson 1995: 308.

church gatherings and a life devoted to profit and planning without consideration of God on other days. But Miriam Kamell reminds us that "James's understanding of humility is *not* a wholesale condemnation of those with means but is rather the basis for his economic ethics. His condemnation of the merchants was not that they failed to give their money to the poor but that they failed to be humble before God."[159] At the same time, James ends his instructions to the merchants by encouraging them to do right. In the context of James, doing right is not only asking for God's wisdom and consulting God in all areas of life, it is also caring for the widow and orphan. In other words, profit cannot be pursued at the expense of those in need. For decades, business in the United States lived by the mantra that shareholder profits had to be maximized to the exclusion of many other societal goods. According to Steven Pearlstein,

> Maximizing shareholder value has meant doing whatever is necessary to boost the share price this quarter and the next. Over the years, it has been used to justify bamboozling customers, squeezing workers and suppliers, avoiding taxes and lavishing stock options on executives. Most of what people find so distasteful about American capitalism—the ruthlessness, the greed, the inequality—has its roots in this misguided notion about what business is all about.[160]

Even corporations have now come to see that the goal of profit at the expense of all else is unsustainable. Instead, more corporations are intent on producing value for customers, dealing fairly with customers and suppliers, protecting the environment, and other social goods.[161] As Christians involved in business, it is appropriate to do what is right for employees, customers, neighbors, and those in need as part of good business practices that recognize the need for faith and works to come together with humility in the practice of business.

Condemnation of the Rich (James 5:1–6)

As in 4:13, James begins this section with the words "come now." But while the previous section was addressed to wealthy merchants, this section is

---

159. Kamell 2009: 171.
160. Pearlstein 2019.
161. Denning 2019.

Commentary

addressed to "the rich." We have already encountered the rich several times in the book of James. We first come across them in Jas 1:9–10, where they were instructed to boast in their lowly position and their pursuits are compared to the tiny, transitory grass flowers that last for a day and disappear. Jas 1:9–10 is ambiguous about whether or not the rich person depicted is a "brother," part of the Christian community. However, as we read further in James, the rich are described as people who oppress the members of the community, drag them into court, and mock the name by which James's readers are known (2:6–7). Now, in this passage the rich are described as those who steal from their workers, hoard wealth for themselves, live in luxury without regard for others, and murder the righteous. James Coker put it this way:

> What the wealthy have and have *not* done with their wealth condemns them utterly and "cries out against them" (5:4). The lack of imperatives here shows that James is not commanding the wealthy in order for them to change their ways, pay their laborers, and stop living extravagantly.... In 5:1–6, where James employs direct speech to the wealthy, there is no such call for change. There is an unequivocal difference between the [brothers] and the [rich]. In fact, the two imperatives that are used in 5:1 only call for the wealthy to listen ... and weep.... It is clear that [the rich] are not a part of James's audience due to the aggressiveness of his language.[162]

Similarly, Richard Bauckham asserts that the audience of James is not made up of either the rich, a small group of wealthy elite in the Greco-Roman world, nor the destitute but rather of those who would have had at least some means to sustain their ordinary lives and to share with and provide for others.[163] If the rich are not part of the audience that James is addressing, then what we have is a prophetic word that the readers hear as a word that names the reality around them. It is a warning about the judgment of those who abuse others and live arrogantly. Such prophetic words are a form of encouragement to those who are longing for God's justice to be manifest in the world they see.

The instruction that James gives to the rich is to weep. This is not a quiet set of tears but rather tears accompanied by howling or wailing. While the instruction to weep is identical to James's instruction in 4:9, which

---

162. Coker 2015: 150–51.
163. Bauckham 1999: 188.

reads lament, mourn, and *weep*, in 4:9 this instruction takes place within the framework of submission to God, drawing near to God, repentance, and humility. But in 5:1 the instruction to weep is combined with howling or wailing, a word used to describe the reaction of people when God's judgment comes upon them (Hos 7:14; Isa 13:6; 23:1, 6, 14; Jer 48:20). This is the only place in the New Testament where the word "howling" occurs, and it is associated with God's judgment of the rich. They are howling because the lives of ease that they once lived will be filled with misery. Again, in contrast with 4:9 where the verbal form of "misery" means lament and pertains to their attitude towards sin, here "miseries" refers to the judgment that is coming. The very things that they have relied upon have rotted and their clothes have been eaten by moths (5:2). The gold and silver that seemed indestructible have rusted, making them worthless. And the clothes that marked their status as people of wealth have been destroyed by moths. Alicia Batten remarks that these clothes are indicators of greedy gain at the expense of others.[164]

In verses 3–4, James uses personification. The rust that has destroyed their wealth is a witness against the rich, and the rust itself eats the flesh of the rich (v. 3). James adds a simile to this description when he says that the rust eats their flesh *like* fire. And in verse 4, a further personification describes the stolen wage itself as crying out. These strong images depict the ruined and stolen wealth as sources of accusation against the unjust practices of the rich. Not only is the wealth described as corroded, but it eats their flesh. This vivid description conjures up flames licking at the bodies of the wealthy. Immediately, James makes a statement: they have stored up treasure for themselves in the last days. This saying is reminiscent of Matt 6:19–21: "Do not store up for yourselves treasure on earth, where moth and rust destroys and where thieves break in and steal; but store up for yourselves treasure in heaven, where neither moth nor rust destroy and where thieves do not break in nor steal; for where your treasure is, there also your heart will be." While the saying in James is much shorter, it highlights the decision that this group has made to hoard wealth for themselves during their earthly lives. James uses the language of "the last days" to describe the time period in which the wealthy are living. Throughout the New Testament "the last days" refers to the period that begins with the death and resurrection of Jesus and extends to Jesus's return when God's justice will be fully realized. James indicates that when the attention of the rich should

---

164. Batten 2009: 488.

Commentary

be on the imminent end, they are instead storing up treasure that is useless in God's kingdom.

Verse 4 opens with the instruction "Behold!" This sharp interjection instructs the audience to pay attention. What is it they are to look at? They are to look at the wages that have been stolen from the workers who mowed the fields of the wealthy. It is only at the end of the clause that James announces that the wage is one that has been taken by fraud. The rich who are depicted in this text are wealthy landowners who hire laborers to mow the fields only to withhold their rightful wages. Maynard-Reid writes:

> It should be noted that the problem of large landowners dominating the economic scene of the first century was a matter of concern to more than just the biblical writers. Seneca, the Roman writer who lived from 4 BC to AD 65, denounced avarice and human craving for overmuch as the cause of poverty—a craving which brought an end to the happy age of communal existence. He then goes on to show how this *avaritia* brought oppression to the poor and added estate to estate of the big landowner: "She adds one estate to another, evicting a neighbor either by buying him out or by wronging him.... She extends her country-seats to the size of provinces and defines ownership as meaning extensive travel through one's own property."
>
> This state of affairs was not limited to Italy, but in other places thousands of farmers were tilling and digging to fill *one* "single belly." Empire-wide there was an increasing concentration of rural wealth in the hands of just a few. Numerous cruel pressures were exerted by the strong landowners against the weak, by "the arrogant rich, 'the powerful,' against the adjoining farm, villagers, or 'the poor,' sometimes by crooked litigation, sometimes by armed force" (emphasis and ellipsis original).[165]

It is these wages stolen from the agricultural laborer that cry out, and these cries are heard by God whose name is "Lord of the Armies," Lord Sabaoth. Sabaoth is a transliteration of the Hebrew word for armies. And James depicts God as the leader of a host, whether human or angelic, that will bring judgment on those who have oppressed the poor. The only other New Testament use of this description of God is in Rom 9:29, where it is found in a quotation from Isaiah. This description of God was a favorite of Isaiah's, who used it almost fifty times in his prophetic book. At least one of these relates directly to the rich who oppress the poor. Isaiah 5:8–9 states, "Ah,

---

165. Maynard-Reid 1987: 86.

you who join house to house, who add field to field, until there is room for no one but you, and you are left to live alone in the midst of the land! The LORD of hosts has sworn in my hearing: Surely many houses shall be desolate, large and beautiful houses without inhabitant." The rich who have defrauded their workers and lived in arrogant luxury (5:5) can expect the judgment of the Lord of Hosts. While their workers lack wages, the rich are engaged in conspicuous consumption. The rich fatten their hearts in the day of slaughter. The "day of slaughter" is a vivid way of referring to the judgment of God that will take place on the last day. Moo notes:

> The rich are selfishly and ignorantly going about accumulating wealth for themselves and wastefully spending it on their own pleasures in the very day when God's judgment is imminently threatened. The "last days" have already begun; the judgment *could* break in at any time—yet the rich, instead of acting to avoid that judgment, are, by their selfish indulgence, incurring greater guilt. They are like cattle being fattened for the kill.[166]

Verse 6 brings James's final accusation. They have passed sentence on and murdered the righteous one, and that righteous one was a person who did not resist their injustice. The singular "righteous one" has been understood in several ways. The two most prominent are: first, as a reference to the collective group of workers who were stripped of their justly earned wages; second, as a reference to Jesus, especially to his submission to arrest and crucifixion. In this context, the first reference is the more likely; nothing prepares the reader for the introduction of Jesus here, but it is certainly possible that James alludes to Jesus at the same time so that the mistreated workers are identified with the mistreatment of the Lord. The apocryphal book the Wisdom of Solomon suggests the way in which the rich may oppress and murder the righteous poor:

> 6 "Come, therefore, let us enjoy the good things that exist,
>   and make use of the creation to the full as in youth.
> 7 Let us take our fill of costly wine and perfumes,
>   and let no flower of spring pass us by.
> 8 Let us crown ourselves with rosebuds before they wither.
> 9 Let none of us fail to share in our revelry;
>   everywhere let us leave signs of enjoyment,
>   because this is our portion, and this our lot.
> 10 Let us oppress the righteous poor man;

---

166. Moo 2000: 219.

Commentary

> let us not spare the widow
> or regard the gray hairs of the aged.
> 11 But let our might be our law of right,
> for what is weak proves itself to be useless.
> 12 Let us lie in wait for the righteous man,
> because he is inconvenient to us and opposes our actions;
> he reproaches us for sins against the law,
> and accuses us of sins against our training." (Wis. 2:6-12)

The wealthy landowners are described as abusing their power in order to gain at the expense of others. The ultimate outcome is death and destruction. It is possible that this death comes about directly through such actions as imprisonment or that the murderous outcome is the indirect outcome of lack of wages—the inability to provide food and shelter that leads to death.

Fusing the Horizons

Whenever I have taught the book of James, someone asks after discussing Jas 5:1-6, "Is it impossible for rich people to be saved?" Or, the question might be, "Are all rich people evil?" I often respond by suggesting that different questions and perspectives might help us understand James 5:1-6 for our times. Richard Bauckham writes,

> The propensity of the rich to ignore the poor is not only an ethical but also a religious matter. To truly confront the plight of the poor would disturb the rich in their comfortable cocooning of themselves against the realities of life. . . . The illusions of affluence are virtually the religion of contemporary western society. Its spiritual malaise cannot be cured without profound and practical attention to the destitute. . . . If such [statistics about poverty] defy the imagination, then we should think concretely of some of these poorest of people—such as the street children of Rio de Janeiro or those who live on the rubbish tips of Manila: these are the orphans and widows of today's global village. These are the destitute. . . . It is these whom God has chosen to inherit the kingdom (2:5).[167]

But I think we must go beyond considering or even helping the poor. Instead, we might ask how this passage is good news for the poor. Elsa Tamez's work from the Latin American perspective points out that "a Latin American reading of the epistle . . . fixes its gaze on the oppressed and

---

167. Bauckham 1999: 190-91.

James

dedicates long pages to them, their sufferings, complaints, oppression, hope, and praxis."[168] In that context, we might note the following ways that this passage is good news for the poor. God despises those who steal from their workers. God despises fraud. God hears the pleas of those who have been misused and deceived. God's judgment of the oppressive rich is reliable and a source of hope for the poor. The poor can trust that the Lord of Armies who has promised God's kingdom to the poor will indeed bring about his kingdom, and they will find their favored place with God. This is indeed good news for the poor. And for the rich who also want to enter God's kingdom, we (I count myself among them) must find ways to learn from and walk alongside the poor, not as their helpers but as disciples of those who have learned to be rich in faith (2:5).

Patient Anticipation of the Lord's Return (James 5:7-12)

The "therefore" and the return to the direct address "brothers and sisters" signals that James is once again addressing the community of Christians—no longer talking about merchants and wealthy landowners but instead addressing his audience who are struggling to live faithfully within the broader dispersion. The previous passage (5:1-6) serves as a reassurance for James's audience that the greedy excesses of the rich that bring about oppression and injustice for others will not be allowed to continue indefinitely. Now, James turns his attention to the Christian brothers and sisters and instructs them in patient endurance. They are to wait for the coming of the Lord. James reminds them that the end of time, when God will return and set everything right, is near at hand. In this section, James gives several examples of those who wait and endure. Sandwiched between those examples is the instruction not to grumble or complain against each other. And the section ends with a focus on integrity in speech. Once again, the manner of speech within the community is an important component of James's wisdom about right living in the midst of a world where oppression and injustice is a real possibility.

James 5:11 begins with the imperative "be patient." While the word for patience does occur in the Greek literature of James's day, the real depth of its meaning for Christians is derived from its use in the Old Testament where it describes one of the characteristics of God.[169] In Exod 34:6 God

168. Tamez 2002: 21.
169. *TDNT*, 4:379.

Commentary

declares about himself that he is "compassionate and merciful, *patient* and very merciful and truthful" (NETS, emphasis added). When Christians demonstrate patience in the face of injustice, this is not simply hanging in there or drumming up self-control in a situation they can do nothing about. To simply exercise self-control in the face of injustice can be a form of stoicism. Instead, Christian patience in the face of injustice is both a reflection of God's character and a sign of the God in whom the community has placed its hope. Indeed, the brothers and sisters are to exercise patience "until the coming of the Lord." The word for "coming" (*parousia*) at its root means "presence." Those who are waiting patiently are anticipating the time when the Lord will be fully present with them, thus, his coming. This most likely refers to the second coming of Jesus. No one knows exactly when this will happen (Matt 24:36), but it will take place suddenly (Matt 24:27). Until that time, Christians understand that God is the one who helps them to live in ways that demonstrate the distinctive work of God in their lives (1 Thess 5:23). Patience is the hopeful way of life that Christians demonstrate as they look forward to the day when Jesus will be fully present with them, and they know that in that day Jesus will set all things right.

To further encourage them, James illustrates patience with the picture of a farmer who waits for rain. There are two possible backgrounds to the description of the rains in this passage. The Old Testament talks about the early and the later rains. For example, Deut 11:14, "Then he will give the rain for your land in its season, the early rain and the later rain, and you will gather in your grain, your wine, and your oil." Or, "O children of Zion, be glad and rejoice in the LORD your God; for he has given the early rain for your vindication, he has poured down for you abundant rain, the early and the later rain as before. The threshing floors shall be full of grain, the vats shall overflow with wine and oil" (Joel 2:23–24). These verses link the provision of the rains with the abundance of the harvest. Israel had to wait patiently for the Lord to provide the rain so that they could experience the abundant harvest. There was no river like the Nile or the Euphrates that Israel could rely on. Instead, patient waiting for the Lord's provision was part of Israel's demonstration of trust in God's faithfulness. In addition, James was a person who knew the rainy and dry seasons that are characteristic of Palestine. Indeed, "Throughout the Mediterranean, the climate is marked by winter rains and summer droughts.... Winter begins in mid-October, when the rains begin, and lasts through the end of April."[170] In the context

---

170. Fiensy and Strange 2014: 301.

where Christians are being asked to wait patiently for the coming of the Lord even when they see or experience injustice, the picture of the farmer who waits for the rain is significant. Rain is outside the control of the farmer. The farmer must trust that the rain needed to grow the crops that will sustain the family and the community for the year ahead will come. Similarly, the Christians who wait must trust that the Lord will come. The farmer cannot rush to harvest, he must wait until the later rains that take place in the spring have watered the crop in order to bring it to its peak for an abundant harvest. Then, the harvest occurs, and the fruit that is gathered is precious. Luke Timothy Johnson notes that the word "precious" is usually used to described gem stones and crowns, but here it is applied to fruit.[171] But jewels don't nourish a family. Instead, the patient farmer is able to provide food for his family and community by trusting that the rains will be provided. The fruit of such trusting patience is very precious indeed. And we might also note the difference between the greedy rich who steal the wage that belongs to the harvesters, thus depriving them of their very lives, and the patient farmer who waits for the right time to harvest that which is his and finds that harvest to be precious. Like the patient, trusting farmer, the brothers and sisters in the community are also to practice hopeful, trusting patience. At the beginning of verse 8, James repeats the imperative, "be patient," that began this section. He then adds a second imperative, "Strengthen your hearts." Peter Davids describes this as "meaning to stand firmly in the faith, not to give way to doubt."[172] In a verse that shares several similar themes to James, Paul writes, "And may [the Lord] so *strengthen* your hearts in holiness that you may be blameless before our God and Father *at the coming of our Lord* Jesus with all his saints" (1 Thess 3:13, emphasis added). The brothers and sisters are not just to wait patiently but are to actively establish their hearts in the faith. For James (and Paul), establishing one's heart involves a holiness of life and the joining of faith and good works, such as visiting those in need (Jas 1:27). The reason that James gives for their patience and firmness in the faith is that they know that the Lord's return is near. In the New Testament, the word "near" often refers to being near in time and means "to be near, very near, but not yet arrived."[173] This is the judgment that takes place on the day of the Lord, and that day is still to come. James is referring to the nearness of Jesus's second

---

171. Johnson 1995: 315.
172. Davids 1982: 185.
173. McKnight 2011: 413.

Commentary

coming and to the judgment Jesus will undertake that is a necessary part of setting the world to rights.

> *Eschatology in James:* The second coming of Jesus is the completion of the work that Jesus began on the cross when he initially defeated the power of sin and overcame Satan and the demonic forces. In his resurrection, Jesus demonstrates the ultimate defeat of death itself. Scholars refer to this initial defeat of sin, death, and the powers of darkness at the cross and resurrection as "inaugurated eschatology." In other words, the beginning of the end times. For now, Christians, including the Christians addressed by James, live in the "last days" because that last time era began with the cross and resurrection. But Christians, including those addressed by James, also anticipate the second coming when Jesus will ultimately judge sin and wickedness and the forces of evil and set all things right through his justice and mercy. While James and the first generation of Christians expected this event to take place in their lifetime, the length of time between the cross and the second coming is unknown.[174] Christians already live with the inbreaking realities of the kingdom of God demonstrated through Jesus's death on the cross and his resurrection, and that new reality allows Christians to believe that God is the one true God, to live as people who care for the poor, and to pursue friendship with God through a holy life in both word and deed while also anticipating that the time for judgment draws near. One of the features of that judgment is radical reversal—the poor lifted up, the rich made low. James's identification of "the rich" as one group and the "brothers and sisters" as another group invites the question, "With which group will one find oneself at the coming of Jesus?" Here, it may be helpful to remember that not everyone will experience judgment in the same way. For those like "the rich" of Jas 5:1–6, who have oppressed others in order to live in luxury, the judgment will be quite different than for those who have sought the way of righteousness and humility. The brothers and sisters of James's audience receive the assurance that while God is the judge, he is also full of mercy and compassion (5:11).

It might seem that the instructions related to speech in Jas 5:9 are out of place, and that perhaps they are simply another iteration of the theme of right speech (1:27; 3:1–12; 4:11–12) that has been so prominent in the

---

174. Moo 2000: 226 takes this view in his commentary.

book of James. Martin Dibelius, who generally sees the sayings in James as isolated units, also takes this verse as an isolated saying.[175] But more recent scholars see this instruction as one that is embedded in the context of patient waiting for the Lord's return. Many note that there is a temptation when waiting with expectation for something as momentous as the return of the Lord to become short tempered with those around. And indeed, James turns his attention from instructing them to be patient and wait to reminding them of how they are to treat others within their community while they wait. They are not to complain about or against each other. The word *stenazō* can also mean to "groan" and "sigh," and these are the outward expressions of the inward complaints that they may have. Douglas Moo notes that elsewhere in the Bible "groaning" is used in the context of oppressive circumstances, such as the groaning that takes place when the Israelites are oppressed by Pharoah (Exod 2:23). Here, the complaining that is to be avoided within the Christian community is the same kind of groaning that also occurs in the context of oppression.[176] The reason they are not to complain against each other is so that they may not be judged.

The topic of judging and judges has come up numerous times in James. In 2:4, James points to their show of partiality as an example of becoming judges with evil thoughts. And in 4:11–12, James specifically instructs that they are not to slander or judge each other because doing so places the person who acts in this way above the law (the Old Testament Torah or instruction). James has already reminded them that there is one law giver and one judge (4:12) and that the true judge and lawgiver is the one with the power to save and destroy. So, when James tells them not to complain against one another, he once again taps into the themes of speech, judging, and the true judge. Good speech in James is speech that is deliberate (1:19), peaceable (3:17), and demonstrates friendship with God (4:4). Complaining against others is one more example of the kind of speech that causes division and discord in the community (4:1–2). God cannot allow this kind of speech, which destroys his people, to go unjudged. James reminds them that the judge, the one with the power to save and to destroy, is standing at the door. There is a certain nearness expressed in this image. Just on the other side of the door, the door which may swing open at any moment, the judge is standing. Once again, this raises the question for the reader, "When the door is opened, do you expect to find yourself on the side of salvation

---

175. Dibelius 1975: 245.
176. Moo 2000: 226.

Commentary

or of destruction?" Those who choose complaining may want to reconsider in light of God's forthcoming judgment, a judgment directed both at those outside the community and those within it.

For the third time in this short passage (5:7–11), James addresses them as brothers and sisters, reiterating their family identity. This family is to take for their example the prophets. James gives two identifying features of prophets. First, they are people who have experienced suffering and the need for endurance. While the Old Testament does not indicate that every prophet suffered, some certainly did. Many suffered because those to whom they were sent did not listen to the message that God communicated through the prophet. For example, the prophet Micaiah predicted that Ahab, king of Israel, would die in battle and that his armies would be scattered on the mountains. The king's response was to order, "Put this fellow in prison, and feed him on reduced rations of bread and water until I return in peace" (2 Chr 18:26). Some of the prophets are especially well known for the suffering they endured. The prophet Jeremiah was beaten and put in stocks by the priest Pashhur (Jer 20:1–2). Later in his prophetic ministry, he prophesied about the destruction of Jerusalem and urged people to flee for their lives. Those in power saw this as discouraging the soldiers and the people of the city, so they threw him into a muddy cistern where he began to sink into the mud (Jer 38:1–6). Jeremiah also suffered because the people to whom he brought God's message did not repent. Instead, he himself lamented the sins of his people (e.g., Jer 13:17). By the time of the New Testament, a tradition had arisen that many of the prophets suffered martyrdom. Dibelius points out, "One must keep in mind how common the notion of the prophets as martyrs was during this period. . . . Jesus and the Christians put special emphasis upon this idea . . . by recalling the misdeeds of the Jews against the prophets (cf. Matt 5:12; 23:29–39; Mark 12:1ff)."[177] James does not put any special emphasis on the death of the prophets but instead focuses on their endurance in the face of suffering. Second, these prophets were people who spoke in the name of the Lord. They communicated messages that came from God in contrast to false prophets who spoke of their own volition and for their own purposes. The community are to consider the prophets as an example that encourages them to persevere in the midst of suffering.

James 5:7–11 begins with the repeated instruction (5:7, 8) to have patience. Now, James reminds them that "we consider those who endure

---

177. Dibelius 1975: 245–46.

blessed." In chapter 1, there are two types of people who are blessed: the one who endures trials (and/or temptations) (1:12) and the one who looks into the perfect law and puts it into practice (1:25). Now, using the verb, James associates himself with his audience by saying "we" to indicate that both the author and audience think that those who endure are blessed or honored both by God and by the community. In this way, James once again lifts up those who endure. He then turns to the final example in this section, Job. The brothers and sisters are invited to remember the endurance of Job. Readers of the Old Testament book of Job might be forgiven for thinking that Job is not necessarily the model of patience. After all, this is the man who refused to listen to his friends who observed his loss of wealth, family, and health and were convinced that he must have sinned against God. Instead, Job insisted on his innocence and was determined to make the case for his innocence before God. James is probably the writer who most clearly connects Job with the theme of patient endurance.[178] Over time, various traditions that are not included in the biblical text became associated with particular biblical characters as their stories were retold both orally and in writing. One of the retellings of Job's story can be found in the Testament of Job. The genre of "testament" is one that relies on the idea that during a final illness, one of the great patriarchs passes on wisdom from his life to the next generation.[179] Peter Davids notes that the Testament of Job, like the book of James, also emphasizes Job's patient endurance. The complaints that are found on the lips of the canonical Job are now in the Testament of Job complaints made by Job's wife. And the testing that Job undergoes is seen as a test of Job's faithfulness to God.[180] While it's impossible to say whether James knew of the Testament of Job, it is plausible to recognize that one of the emphases that seems to have grown up around the story of Job is the idea that Job faithfully endured the catastrophes that happened to him. James says, "You heard of the endurance of Job and you saw the end of the Lord." While the phrase "the end of the Lord" is vague, it most likely refers to the conclusion of Job's narrative. After Job's endurance, he experiences both vindication and restoration. In Job 40–42, God is revealed in a terrible whirlwind and Job is humbled. The friends are instructed to ask Job to pray

---

178. Johnson 1995: 320.

179. The Testament of Job was written sometime between 100 BCE and 100 CE. Similar testaments include Testaments of the Twelve Patriarchs, Testament of Moses, and The Testament of Abraham.

180. Davids 1982: 188.

for them. And Job's health, wealth, and family are restored. James reminds his readers that they have not only seen the human endurance of Job but also seen the Lord's response to Job's patient, faithful endurance of suffering. James ends his instruction on patience and endurance with a reminder that the Lord is very compassionate and merciful. The word translated "very compassionate" (*polusplagxnos*) only occurs here in the biblical text. The compound word, great-compassion, highlights the fullness and expansiveness of God's compassion. This is followed by a reminder that God is merciful. The only other use of the word "merciful" (*oiktirmōn*) in the New Testament is found in Luke 6:36, where Jesus says, "Be merciful, just as your Father is merciful." This may once again echo the description of God in Exod 34:6 as one who is merciful, patient, and truthful. The brothers and sisters who have observed corruption and arrogance and perhaps been impacted by it are instructed to wait patiently for the coming of Jesus, to speak with grace towards one another, and to look to the Jewish examples of endurance for encouragement while being reminded that God is ultimately a God of compassion and mercy who deals justly with his people.

Integrity in Speech (James 5:12)

It is hard to determine if James 5:12 should be its own separate section or whether it belongs with either what has come before (5:7–11) or what comes after (5:13–18). It begins with the words "but above all" and the direct address "my brothers and sisters," then changes topic with the instruction that they should not swear an oath. Many commentators note these markers as signs that this verse stands alone as its own unit.[181] Others note that the verse ends with a reason for not swearing oaths: namely, "so that you may not fall under judgment." These scholars suggest that the theme of God's righteous judgment in the last day continues here and that v. 12 rightly belongs with 5:7–11 because it shares that theme of God's judgment.[182] Still others think that Jas 5:12 is the starting point for the end of the letter. Johnson notes that the phrase "above all" can mark the end of an epistle and that the use of the negative "do not" (*mē*) has marked the opening of other portions of the letter (2:1; 3:1; 4:11).[183] The verse serves as a transition here, at the end of the letter, between the focus on the judgment that is part of

---

181. Allison 2013: 727–28; Davids 1982: 189; Dibelius 1975: 251.
182. Penner 1996: 150.
183. Johnson 1995: 326–27.

James

Christ's coming, a reminder yet again of the theme of right speech within the community, and a turn to communal care for one another that we will see in Jas 5:13–20. It is hard to determine the exact starting point for the end of James's letter since it does not follow the conventions we are familiar with for letter endings either from our reading of the Pauline epistles or from our reading of Greco-Roman epistles. But it is clear as we approach this verse that we are nearing the end of the epistle.

> *The Words of Jesus in the Book of James:* By this point in the book of James, it is clear that the name of Jesus only appears twice (1:1; 2:1). But instead of thinking that the book of James is not concerned with Jesus's message, it is important to realize that the teachings of Jesus are found throughout the epistle. James never says something like, "As Jesus says . . ." Instead, Jesus's influence is felt in the way that James makes the teachings of Jesus his own and passes them on to his audience. We can see that the book of James and the Gospels share a common understanding of some of the teachings and sayings of Jesus. Here, Jas 5:12 reads, "Above all, my beloved, <u>do not swear, either by heaven,</u> or <u>by earth,</u> or by any other oath, but let your <u>'Yes' be yes</u> and your <u>'No' be no,</u> so that you may not fall under condemnation" (NRSV). This is very similar to what Matt 5:34–37 says, "<u>Do not swear</u> at all, <u>either by heaven,</u> for it is the throne of God, or <u>by the earth,</u> for it is his footstool, or by Jerusalem, for it is the city of the great King. And do not swear by your head, for you cannot make one hair white or black. Let your word be, <u>'Yes, Yes'</u> or <u>'No, No';</u> anything more than this comes from the evil one." The similar parts of these passages are underlined. As contemporary readers, we are used to seeing Matthew, Mark, and Luke at the beginning of the New Testament and reading the chronological story of Jesus's birth, ministry, death, and resurrection. However, we need to remember that it is quite possible that James is written decades before the Gospels. In other words, James may not be quoting from Matthew or another Gospel. Instead, it is quite possible that James knew Jesus's sayings because he heard them in person or he heard oral stories about Jesus teaching or there was an early written source of Jesus's sayings. James takes these sayings of Jesus and makes them his own. Richard Bauckham puts it this way, "As a disciple of Jesus, James was deeply informed by the teaching of his master and made it his own, but, as a wisdom teacher in his own

> right, he reexpressed it and developed it as his own teaching."[184] We see this teaching expressed in themes throughout the book of James. For example, both Jesus and James emphasize joy in tribulation; faith and doubt; warnings about anger; the instruction to love one's neighbor; mercy; and refraining from judgment.[185] When we read the book of James, our awareness of the teaching of Jesus allows us to see both the presence of Jesus in the pages of James and the masterful wisdom of James. We might also be encouraged to think about how drinking deeply from the wisdom of Jesus can enable us to speak wisely to those around us—not by parroting the words of Jesus but by making them deeply our own and then speaking true wisdom to the world around us.

The instruction is clear. "Do not swear an oath." Some translations read "do not swear" (ESV, NASB, NIV), but this can make it sound like James is talking about not using bad words. However, this instruction is about one's allegiance and the integrity of the person who makes an oath. James 5:12 reproduces a saying of Jesus that is also found in Matt 5:33–37. Although the saying is longer in Matthew, they both have a similar structure, the prohibition not to swear, a list of examples of what not to swear by, a demand for integrity in speech, and a reason for the instruction.[186] Both James and Jesus were embedded in a context where people swore oaths by the gods (Romans) or indirectly by other things that were created by God (heaven, earth, temple, etc.). But the Old Testament was clear that Jews should not swear by the name of God (Lev 19:11–13). As Jewish people commented on why they should not swear oaths, they gave a variety of reasons. Sirach says that those who swear oaths will "never be cleansed from sin" and that "the one who swears many oaths is full of iniquity. . . . If he swears in error, his sin remains on him and if he disregards it, he sins doubly; if he swears a false oath, he will not be justified, for his house will be filled with calamities" (Sir 23:10–11 NRSV). In other words, the one who swears a lot of oaths cannot be trusted. Similarly, Philo, who lived around the time of Jesus, writes, "Next to not swearing at all, the second best thing is to keep one's oath; for by the mere fact of swearing at all, the swearer shows that there is some suspicion of his not being trustworthy."[187]

---

184. Bauckham 2019: 11.
185. Bauckham 2019: 10, citing Deppe 1989.
186. Allison 2013: 728.
187. Philo 1993: 84–86.

In other words, Jesus and James, like other Jewish contemporaries, valued the truthfulness and trustworthiness of a person over the giving of an oath, especially an oath that was sworn in God's name or by his creation. Some commentators over the centuries have taken the instruction to not swear an oath completely literally and have forbidden all oath taking, even in courts or other legal circumstances. Others have argued that what is forbidden is bringing dishonor to God's name.[188] Those who have argued for a more literal understanding of the instruction have presented three reasons: "(1) We should tell the truth *at all times*, not just under oath; (2) God, not humans, governs the future, so we should not use oaths to try and force God to act; and (3) we owe ultimate allegiance to God alone, and then to the Christian community, not ultimately to any other social or political community."[189] The reason that James gives for not swearing an oath is "so that you may not fall under judgment." Just as complaining about others in the community leads to a reminder about the judge at the door, so too lack of integrity in speech is joined to a reminder that there is accountability for those whose speech is false and lacking in integrity.

Fusing the Horizons

In some churches, eschatology (the study of the last times) is a topic of prominent discussion while in others it is seldom mentioned. The epistle of James assumes that his audience would have been familiar with important early Christian doctrines including the second coming of the Lord Jesus, the final judgment of humanity, and the mercy and compassion of God towards the followers of Jesus. In James, these doctrines are not so much explained as used to encourage the community to a certain kind of posture and behavior. The posture is one of patient, trusting endurance, and the behavior is one of integrity in speech and, therefore, action. As followers of Jesus, it can be tempting to look back over two thousand years of history with a sense that, since Jesus has not yet returned, there is no need to anticipate his return anytime soon or even in our lifetime. However, just as the early Christians and Jesus himself did not know the day or time, we also do not know the day of his return. In light of that, we too can benefit from remembering that we, like the early Christians, live in the last times, and that the second coming is near in God's time. Contemplating

---

188. Moore-Keish 2019: 185.
189. Moore-Keish 2019: 185.

the return of Christ can be an encouragement to think seriously about the values and priorities of one's life. Is the focus on making money? Getting ahead? Achieving "success" in the eyes of the world? Or is the focus on living faithfully with patience and integrity? Christians do not need to be afraid of God's judgment. The true God is also the one who is able to save. Paul himself talks about the person who builds upon his salvation either with works that will be burned up because they have no value in the eternal world or with works that will last when they face the fire of judgment. Paul reassures the believer that even though the believer passes through judgment, the believers life will be saved no matter what happens (1 Cor 3:10–15). At the same time, awareness of the nearness of God's judgment can be a sobering reminder that God holds believers accountable for the integrity and righteousness of the lives they live. Indeed, James began by asserting that pure religion is demonstrated through visiting those who are vulnerable and keeping oneself pure (Jas 1:27). And throughout his book of wisdom, James returns again and again to the theme of right speech as a significant marker of whether one has kept oneself unstained by the world.

James

Instructions on Prayer (James 5:13–18)

James 5:13–18: Is anyone among you suffering? That one must pray. Is anyone cheerful? That one must sing. (14) Is anyone among you sick? That one must call the elders of the church and they must pray over and anoint that one with oil in the name of the Lord. (15) And the prayer of faith will save the one who is sick and the Lord will raise that one; and if that one has sinned, it will be forgiven. (16) Therefore, confess your sins to one another and pray on behalf of one another, so that you may be healed. The effective prayer of a righteous person is very powerful. (17) Elijah was a man like us, and he prayed fervently that it would not rain, and it did not rain on the earth for three years and six months. (18) And he prayed again, and the heaven gave rain and the earth produced its fruit.

Throughout the book of James, there has been a repeated emphasis on both the individual (anyone) and community (you, plural). This dynamic returns in full force in this section of James, where it is clear that not everyone is experiencing the same thing, but they are all together in community. In this context, James will encourage his readers to pray, sing, participate in God's healing work, and pray some more.

James 5:13 begins with a question, "Is anyone among you suffering?" The verb here is reminiscent of the suffering of the prophets from 5:10. James does not specify the source of the individual's suffering, but from the context of James we might name poverty, prejudice, injustice, abuse by the wealthy and powerful, sickness, and community conflicts (1:9; 2:1–8; 5:14; 4:1–3). Those who suffer are instructed to pray. They are to seek God for relief from all the sources of their suffering. For example, in the Psalms it is clear that the wicked cause suffering for the righteous and the righteous petition God with a voice of trust to care for them in the face of the unjust suffering they experience (e.g., Ps 35). A second question follows: "Is anyone cheerful?" Those who are cheerful are to sing. In the Old and New Testament this singing refers to singing songs of praise. For example, "I will . . . sing praise to the name of the Lord" (Ps 7:17; similarly, Ps 9:2; 13:6; 21:13); other songs of praise to God are sung after the defeat of enemies (Ps 17:6). Such songs could be sung with instruments, so Ps 33:1–3 instructs, "Rejoice in the Lord . . . Praise the Lord with the lyre; make melody to him with the harp of ten strings. Sing to him a new song; play skillfully on the strings, with loud shouts." The Psalms served as a guide for both lament for those who suffered and praise for those who had reason to rejoice.

James 5:14–16 completes the series of questions with, "Is anyone among you sick?" The response to sickness in verse 14–16 generates healing for both the individual and the community. While these verses begin with the individual who is experiencing either chronic or acute sickness, it ends with healing for the whole community (v. 16, "so that you, plural, may be healed"). If an individual is sick, they are to summon or invite the elders of the church to come to them. The word "elders" can refer to older members of the community, the wise leaders of households who helped to guide the community. Such elders were a common feature of Jewish life, and the idea of wise elders who were responsible for the care of the community flowed easily into early Christian life. In the context of James, the elders are most likely leaders of the locally gathered Christians. In the book of Acts, Paul and his companions are described as appointing elders in each church (14:23), and when a debate arose around the necessity of non-Jewish believers being circumcised, Paul and Barnabas were appointed to "go up to Jerusalem to discuss this question with the apostles and the elders" (Acts 15:2). In other words, from the early days of the church, there were leaders who guided the local assemblies. Such persons would be those who were wise and mature. In 1 Tim 5:17 this role is associated with preaching and teaching. These are the elders who are to anoint the sick person with oil in the name of the Lord.

Olive oil was used for a wide variety of purposes in the Mediterranean world, including cosmetic, medicinal, and religious uses. Douglas Moo lays out two potential meanings of "anointing with oil." First, practical uses such as for medicine. Second, religious uses whether sacramental or symbolic. Olive oil was used medicinally in the ancient world, and there is one occasion in Mark where it is associated with healing. When Jesus sent out the twelve, Mark reports that, "They cast out many demons, and anointed with oil many who were sick and cured them" (6:13). While oil is associated with healing the sick both in Mark and in James, it is most likely not a medicine. There were many other forms of medicine in the ancient world, and olive oil was not a cure-all. The religious use of oil was very common in both the Old and New Testaments. Oil was used to consecrate people and set them apart for God. Moo argues that James "would be recommending that the elders anoint the sick person in order vividly to show how that person is being set apart for God's special attention in prayer."[190] The anointing that takes places is a physical action that involves placing oil on the sick person

---

190. Moo 2000: 241.

while praying for them. But note that in James it is the prayer of faith and not the oil itself that is seen as healing.

The prayer of faith is offered by the elders on behalf of the one who is sick. The opening verses of James began with instructions to ask God for wisdom and to ask with faith rather than doubt (1:5–6). Faith is rightly placed in the Lord Jesus (2:1), and true faith in Jesus is demonstrated by one's actions, including good works on behalf of the poor (2:14–17). The prayer of faith by the elders is one that trusts in the Lord Jesus to do the work of healing on behalf of the brother or sister who is sick. This corresponds with the anointing and prayer of Jas 5:14, which is offered "in the name of the Lord." Praying in the name of the Lord is not a magic formula. Rather, it is an acknowledgment of the authority of Jesus to heal those who are sick. In the gospels, we see Jesus frequently healing those who are sick (Luke 4:40) and empowering his followers to heal (Matt 10:8). The prayer of faith "will save." Here James uses the Greek word *sōzō*, which is most frequently translated as "save." This Greek word can mean "to preserve or rescue from natural dangers, save, keep from harm, preserve, rescue," and specifically "to save or free from disease."[191] The word is used this way in the Gospels. For example, a woman with a bleeding disorder says to herself, "If I only touch his cloak, I will be well" (Greek: will be saved, *sōthēsomai*). And when Jesus turns to her, he says, "Your faith has made you well" (Greek: has saved you, *sesōken*). And the woman was well (Greek, was saved, *esōthē*) from that hour (Matt 9:21–22). This is just one example of how healing and wholeness are communicated through the Greek word for "saved" in the Gospels. In the context of people who are described as sick in James, this is its meaning in our verse. At the same time, this Greek word can also refer to being saved from eternal death.[192] It is used with this meaning overwhelmingly in the letters of Paul. For example, in Rom 5:9–10 we read, "Since we have now been justified by his blood, how much more shall we be saved from God's wrath through him! For if, while we were God's enemies, we were reconciled to him through the death of his Son, how much more, having been reconciled, shall we be saved through his life!" (NIV). Throughout James there is a theme of wholeness, and here the use of "will be healed/saved" points to healing in this life. The one who has been in bed will be raised up by the Lord. The word "raised" (*egeirō*) is associated with rising from beds. For example, when Joseph dreams about taking the baby

---

191. BDAG, 982.
192. BDAG, 982.

Commentary

Jesus to Egypt to protect him from Pharoah, he rises and takes the child (Matt 2:14). Or when Peter's mother-in-law was sick in bed, Jesus touched her and she rose (Matt 8:14–15). Or the paralyzed man who arose from his pallet (Matt 9:7). At the same time, the word "raised" is also associated with the resurrection of the dead (e.g., Matt 10:8; 16:21; Rom 6:4; 1 Cor 15:20–22). In the context of James, the focus is on the healing that enables the one who is sick to rise and resume life. Once again, James is clear about who will raise up the one who is sick. It is the Lord, a reference to Jesus, the healer. James ends this verse with the statement, "And if the one who is sick has sinned, that one will be forgiven." Scot McKnight rightly notes that in both the Old and New Testaments sin and sickness were understood in relationship to one another. He writes, "The correlation of sickness with sin and health with covenant faithfulness shapes the core of the Old Testament and of Israel's identity and consciousness."[193] In the New Testament, the disciples assume that the blind man outside the temple must be bearing the consequences of either his own sin or his parents sin; although this is not Jesus's view of the situation since he indicates that the man's blindness is for God's glory (John 9:2). In another gospel story, Jesus forgives the sins of a paralyzed man before healing him, suggesting the intertwining of sin and sickness (Luke 5:17–26). It is important to note the use of "if" in Jas 5:15. Sickness does not have to be correlated with sin, but it is certainly possible that it is correlated with sin. In the context of calling for the elders, being anointed with oil, and receiving prayer, the one who is sick also receives forgiveness of sin if that is needed. When sin is forgiven, God no longer remembers it and the sin no longer has power over the individual.

The focus on the forgiveness of sin for the sick individual leads James to an instruction for the whole community and not just for the one who is sick. Everyone in the community is to confess their sins to one another and to pray on behalf of each other. James does not say much about how this confession to one another works. He does not specify whether this refers to the sick person confessing sin that may be impeding healing. He does not specify whether this confession takes place in public or in a more private setting. He does not specify particular rituals that might accompany the act of confession. Confession here refers to admitting or naming sin. This was a common practice in the Old Testament. In Lev 5:5 the individual is told, "When you realize your guilt in any of these [matters], you shall confess the sin that you have committed." And on the Day of Atonement, the high

---

193. McKnight 2011: 444.

priest confessed sin on behalf of the whole community of Israel (Lev 16:21). Scot McKnight notes that the types of sins that might be confessed can be inferred from the book of James and would include neglect of the poor, sins of speech, abuse or violence towards others, arrogance, and greed.[194] In Dietrich Bonhoeffer's book *Life Together*, there is a whole chapter on "Confession and Communion."[195] In this section of the book Bonhoeffer lays out practical advice for hearing confession of sins in the community. This includes an orientation towards love and forgiveness on the part of the person who hears the confession and the gift of being able to offer restoration to relationship with Christ and relationship with the community to the one who confesses. The outcome of such confession and prayer is healing (*iathēte*). Note that the Greek word used for healing is different here than the Greek word used in 5:15. Both *sōzō* and *iathēte* are used in this passage to refer to physical healing. By using *iathēte* in this context, James makes clear that his reference is to physical healing and not to future salvation from eternal death. Throughout these verses, there has been a focus on prayer. Prayer (*proseuxomai*) is the appropriate response to suffering (5:13) and petitionary prayer (5:14, 15, *euxē*) is the response to sickness. This same petitionary prayer is a regular part of the life of the congregation. They are to petition God on behalf of one another. Just as they anticipate that God will raise up the sick, so too Christian prayer anticipates that God hears and responds to the prayers of God's people. And v. 16 ends with the comment that prayer that comes from a righteous person is very powerful. In James, righteousness is connected with faith that is revealed in both one's words and one's deeds. Those who put their faith into action and who control their tongue will find their petitions more powerful. At the same time, Martha Moore-Keish reminds us, "Our prayers do not come from ourselves alone; they emerge from that word already implanted in us. When we pray, then, we do so out of God's generous grace already at work within us."[196]

In verse 17, James uses another Old Testament character, Elijah, to illustrate effective, faithful prayer. The illustration begins by emphasizing Elijah's humanness: "He was a man like us." In other words, the prayer of faith is not limited to some supposedly super-spiritual person but is rather something that all faithful believers can practice. Very briefly, James retells the story that is found in 1 Kings 17–18. In that story, Elijah tells Ahab, the

---

194. McKnight 2011: 447.
195. Bonhoeffer 1954: 110–22.
196. Moore-Keish 2019: 198.

king of northern Israel that there will be a three-year drought, and then, after three years, is sent back to Ahab to tell him that the drought will come to an end. In the middle of that time period Elijah is provided for through God's miraculous provision for the widow at Zarephath and also raises the son of another widow from death. The Old Testament text assumes Elijah's life of prayer rather than spelling it out explicitly. But by the time of the New Testament, there was a tradition surrounding Elijah that portrayed him as a person of prayer. For example, 2 Esdras (a book written sometime between the first and second century CE) says, "And Elijah [prayed] for those who received the rain, and for the one that was dead that he might live" (7:109). James turns to this example to demonstrate the power and effectiveness of prayer. Elijah prayed and God withheld rain. Elijah prayed again and God gave the rain that brings about the fruitfulness of the earth. It is God who gives and who withholds rain. Elijah is the example James gives of a righteous person whose prayers work powerfully (5:16).

Fusing the Horizons

Prayer is one of the central themes of this passage. Prayer is the conversation we have with God—the act of petitioning God on behalf of others and ourselves, the act of repentance for sin, and the act of listening to God. The one who is experiencing suffering is to share that with the Lord in prayer. Those who are sick are to ask the leaders of the church to come and physically anoint them with oil and pray for them. These prayers are a communal means of intentionally inviting God's care and intervention on behalf of the petitioner. This may include prayer ministry in a variety of forms (for example, prayer chains, healing prayer either in the church or in other locations, and corporate prayers) as well as individual prayer. The Christian community that James envisions contains a variety of individuals who are experiencing different life events—suffering, happiness, and sickness. Similarly, the church today needs to be a place where those who find themselves in very different circumstances all find a place where the realities they are experiencing can be named. The diversity of experiences within the congregation contribute to the diversity of prayer and worship within the community. A major portion of this passage is devoted to prayer for healing. Western culture advocates for health and wholeness in a variety of ways, including seeking help from doctors, therapists, and other health professionals. All of these can be enormously beneficial. At the same time, the church must also be a place where vulnerability is welcome so that healing from both sickness and sin can take place. Some may want to avoid words that they see as having an overly religious meaning, like "sin." But it is also clear that both sins done to individuals and sins committed by individuals can weigh on both mental and physical health. In this context, confessing sin to another mature member of the church or to a pastor and receiving God's promise of forgiveness through that person can contribute to the health and healing of both the individual and the community. Normalizing healing prayer, repentance, and confession contributes to a community where members do not have to hide their weakness, needs, or sins.

We cannot leave this passage without addressing two issues. First, many people have received prayer with or without anointing with oil and have not experienced healing in this life. While James seems to expect that there would indeed be healing, the reality is that such healing does not always happen in this life. We live in a world where death is the consequence of sin, and it is obvious to all of us that sickness and death are ongoing realities of the sinful and fallen world we inhabit. At the same time, Christians who are experiencing sickness should continue to call for the leaders of the church to pray and anoint them with anticipation that Jesus continues to touch and heal in this life. When Christians face the prospect that their sickness is not going to be cured, we must continue to minister to them. Such ministry can first of all involve the ministry of presence along with prayer, listening, and empathy. A simple, "I'm sorry that you have not received the healing you long for," can be a starting point. Another starting point might be to ask, "How can you receive the grace of God in this moment, today?" Second, sometimes when people do not receive healing others have told them that this lack of healing is a lack of faith, that somehow they are responsible for their own sickness because of doubt or not trusting enough. Such a message can be deeply damaging to those who hear it and even cause people to turn away from faith in God. A much more nuanced understanding of sickness, sin, healing, and prayer is needed in the church. As followers of Jesus, we can offer prayer and anointing in the name of Jesus, but it is Jesus, the Lord, who has the sole authority to heal. We do not invoke Jesus's name as a magic formula with a guaranteed response but rather invite with trust and confidence his healing presence in the lives of our sick brothers and sisters. And we can be confident that Jesus can raise us from the sickbed and that he will one day raise all of us from death to life in the new heavens and new earth.

Commentary

Two Ways (James 5:19-20)

James 5:19-20: My brothers and sisters, if anyone among you is wandering from the truth and someone returns him, (20) know that the one who turns a sinner out of his wandering way will save his soul from death and cover a multitude of sins.

James 5:19-20 connects with what comes before by continuing the pattern of addressing an issue that arises for "someone among you." But it is also set apart as the final unit of the book with its use of direct address, "my brothers and sisters," and a turn to a new topic—wandering from the truth. This unit functions as a short conclusion to the letter.[197] It may form a parallel with the opening focus of James on faith and doubt (1:2-8), another section of the letter that focuses on a choice between two ways of living. From the beginning of James, there has been a focus on "the two ways." There is a way of faith, wisdom, and righteousness demonstrated through one's life and speech. And there is a way of doubt, foolishness, and friendship with the world characterized by boasting, quarreling, and conflict. Here, at the conclusion of the book, James uses the imagery of a path and indicates that some members of the community may wander or be led astray from the true and best path. These are individuals within the community who are deceived (see 1:16, which uses the same word) and are choosing a path that leads them away from faith in God, from asking for God's wisdom, and away from friendship with God. Those who stray from the truth are in danger of becoming lost and leaving the community. James already indicated that his audience has been born from God by God's word of truth (1:18). When some within the community wander from the truth, they are turning their back on the one who gave birth to them. They are no longer in a posture of receiving the word that can save (1:21) but are instead turning their backs on the word of truth and its author. In a world where the choice is between friendship with the world or friendship with God; between trust in God or doubt; and between upright behavior and crooked behavior, those who stray from the truth that gave birth to them are aligning themselves with forces opposed to God. Thus, James refers to that person as a sinner—one who rejects God's law of love and chooses the way of the world over the way of God. This one is on a wandering path, specifically wandering from the truth they know and the truth that needs to be lived. James commends the one who turns such a person back. The

---

197. Other scholars think that the conclusion to the book starts at 5:7 or at 5:13.

image of turning also contributes to the picture of a path with two ways, a way that heads towards truth, and thus towards God, and a way pointed away from truth, towards the world and the devil. The one who is turning the wanderer is not seeking "conversion"—after all, the person is already part of the Christian community—but rather a return to a life that is in line with the truth by which they first became part of God's family of brothers and sisters. Such a return to truth is conveyed through wisdom, alignment with God, and practices that pursue care for the needy, peace, and mercy.

With a final imperative, James reminds the audience that there are two things that they know: first, the one who turns back a person who is wandering "will save his soul from death." Second, such turning "will cover a multitude of sins." The "soul" refers to the whole person and not to a separate "spiritual" part of someone's being. The one who wanders from the truth is in danger of dying and experiencing God's final judgment. To return to truth is to return to God, to the one who gives birth, sustains life, and provides wisdom. Such a return implies the forgiveness of sins. And James says that the one who turns a sinner from his wandering path will cover a multitude of sins. This is most likely an allusion to Proverbs 10:12, "Hatred stirs up strife, but love covers all offenses." Martha Moore-Keish notes that "covering sins" is not about hiding sin or pretending it doesn't exist but is instead about forgiveness.[198] It is interesting here, at the very end of the book, that James does not specifically indicate that the forgiveness that the wanderer receives comes from God. Instead, it is in the context of the brother or sister who pursues the wanderer that forgiveness takes place. As Bonhoeffer puts it, "The sinner surrenders; he gives up all his evil. He gives his heart to God, and he finds the forgiveness of all his sin in the fellowship of Jesus Christ and his brother. The expressed, acknowledged sin has lost all its power. It has been revealed and judged as sin."[199] James does not tell us whether the one who wandered returned or whether the one who tries to turn the wanderer was effective. But he closes his book with a picture of a path and a choice between two ways.[200] And he closes his book with the picture of a community that seeks out those who wander.

---

198. Moore-Keish 2019: 202.

199. Bonhoeffer 1954: 112–13.

200. I am indebted to my student Benjamin McCully for his observations about the two ways in James 5:19–20.

Fusing the Horizons

From the very beginning of James, the audience has been presented with a choice between two ways. Now, as the book draws to a close, the reader is once again presented with a choice—choosing the path towards God or away from God; choosing the way of attempting to turn the wanderer or of ignoring the wanderer. The repeated focus on two ways in this book reminds us that each day we are on a journey and that each day we choose the direction that journey will take us. Those of us who have been born anew through the word of truth are invited each and every day to live to the best of our ability as friends of God who pursue the truth implanted in God's people. We pursue this truth through our actions, our speech, and our attitudes. We seek peace, generosity towards others, and care for the vulnerable. And we are aware that it is God who generously gives to us the wisdom and strength that are needed to live in friendship with God, to pursue the path of truth, and to live with care for God's community.

BIBLIOGRAPHY

Adamson, James B. 1976. *The Epistle of James.* The New International Commentary on the New Testament. Grand Rapids: Eerdmans.
Allison, Dale C. 2013. *A Critical and Exegetical Commentary on the Epistle of James.* New York: Bloomsbury.
Barclay, John M. G. 2015. *Paul and the Gift.* Grand Rapids: Eerdmans.
———. 2020. *Paul and the Power of Grace.* Grand Rapids: Eerdmans.
Batten, Alicia J. 2009. "Neither Gold nor Braided Hair (1 Timothy 2:9; 1 Peter 3:3): Adornment, Gender and Honour in Antiquity." *New Testament Studies* 55:484–501.
———. 2010. *Friendship and Benefaction in James.* Emory Studies in Early Christianity 15. Atlanta: Society of Biblical Literature.
Bauckham, Richard. 1999. *James.* New Testament Readings. London: Routledge.
———. 2004. *Jude and the Relatives of Jesus in the Early Church.* London: T&T Clark.
———. 2019. "James and Jesus Traditions." In *Reading the Epistle of James: A Resource for Students*, edited by Eric F. Mason and Darian R. Lockett, 9–26. Atlanta: SBL.
Bauer, W., et al., eds. 2000. *A Greek-English Lexicon of the New Testament and Other Early Christian Literature.* 3rd ed. Accordance electronic ed. Chicago: University of Chicago Press.
Blomberg, Craig L. 1992. *Matthew.* Edited by E. Ray Clendenen and David S. Dockery. Accordance electronic ed. New American Commentary 22. Nashville: Broadman & Holman.
Bonhoeffer, Dietrich. 1954. *Life Together.* New York: Harper Collins.
Bottaro, Angelica. 2023. "Cyberbullying: Everything You Need to Know." *Verywell Health*, Oct. 6. https://www.verywellhealth.com/cyberbullying-effects-and-what-to-do-5220584.
Bowden, Andrew. 2014. "Count What All Joy?: The Translation of Πειρασμός in James 1.2 and 12." *The Bible Translator* 65:113–24.
Boyce, James L. 2015. "A Mirror of Identity: Implanted Word and Pure Religion in James 1:17–27." *Word and World* 35:213–21.
Brown, Francis, et al., eds. 1906. *The Brown-Driver-Briggs Hebrew and English Lexicon.* Accordance electronic ed. Oxford: Clarendon.
Calvin, John, and John King. 1847. *Calvin's Commentaries (Complete).* Accordance electronic ed. Edinburgh: Calvin Translation Society.
Charles, R. H. 1913. *The Apocrypha and Pseudepigrapha of the Old Testament.* Edited by Joshua Williams. Oxford: Clarendon.

Bibliography

Clines, David J. A. 1997. *The Theme of the Pentateuch*. Edited by Philip R. Davies. Journal for the Study of the Old Testament Supplement Series 10. Sheffield: Sheffield Academic.

Coker, K. Jason. 2015. *James in Postcolonial Perspective: The Letter as Nativist Discourse*. Minneapolis: Fortress.

Corbett, Steve, and Brian Fikkert. 2009. *When Helping Hurts: How to Alleviate Poverty without Hurting the Poor . . . and Yourself*. Chicago: Moody.

Davids, Peter H. 1982. *The Epistle of James: A Commentary on the Greek Text*. New International Greek Testament Commentary. Grand Rapids: Eerdmans.

———. 1989. *James*. New International Biblical Commentary. Peabody: Hendrickson.

Denning, Steve. 2019. "Why Maximizing Shareholder Value Is Finally Dying." *Forbes*, Aug. 19. https://www.forbes.com/sites/stevedenning/2019/08/19/why-maximizing-shareholder-value-is-finally-dying.

Deppe, Dean. 1989. *The Sayings of Jesus in the Epistle of James*. Parker: Bookcrafters.

deSilva, David A. 2000. "Patronage." In *Dictionary of New Testament Background*, edited by Craig A. Evans and Stanley E. Porter, 767. Downers Grove: InterVarsity.

Dibelius, Martin. 1975. *James: A Commentary on the Epistle of James*. Hermeneia. Philadelphia: Augsburg Fortress.

Fiensy, David A., and James R. Strange. 2014. *Galilee in the Late Second Temple and Mishnaic Periods: Life, Culture, and Society*. Galilee in the Late Second Temple and Mishnaic Periods. Minneapolis: Fortress.

Hanson, K. C. 1994. "How Honorable! How Shameful! A Cultural Analysis of Matthew's Makarisms and Reproaches." *Semeia* 68:81–111.

Hartin, P. J. 1999. *A Spirituality of Perfection: Faith in Action in the Letter of James*. Collegeville: Liturgical.

Hockey, Katherine M. 2019. *The Role of Emotion in 1 Peter*. Society for New Testament Studies Monograph Series 173. New York: Cambridge University Press.

Jackson-McCabe, Matt A. 2001. "The Law of Freedom (James 1:25): Light from Early Exegesis." *Proceedings* 21:33–44.

Johnson, Luke Timothy, ed. 1995. *The Letter of James: A New Translation with Introduction and Commentary*. Anchor Bible 37A. New York: Doubleday.

Josephus, Flavius. 1987. *The Works of Josephus: Complete and Unabridged*. Peabody: Hendrickson.

Kamell, Mariam. 2009. "The Economics of Humility: The Rich and the Humble in James." In *Engaging Economics: New Testament Scenarios and Early Christian Reception*, edited by Bruce W. Longenecker and Kelly D. Liebengood, 157–75. Grand Rapids: Eerdmans.

Keener, Craig S. 2014. *The IVP Bible Background Commentary: New Testament*. 2nd ed. Downers Grove: InterVarsity.

Laws, Sophie. 1993. *The Epistle of James*. Black's New Testament Commentaries. Peabody: Hendrickson.

Levenson, Jon D. 1998. "Abusing Abraham: Traditions, Religious Histories, and Modern Misinterpretations." *Judaism* 47.3:259–77.

Lockett, Darian R. 2008. *Purity and Worldview in the Epistle of James*. Library of New Testament Studies 366. New York: T&T Clark.

Longenecker, Bruce W. 2009. "Exposing the Economic Middle: A Revised Economy Scale for the Study of Early Urban Christianity." *Journal for the Study of the New Testament* 31:243–78.

Martin, Ralph P. 1988. *James*. Word Biblical Commentary 48. Waco: Word.

Bibliography

Maynard-Reid, Pedrito U. 1987. *Poverty and Wealth in James*. Maryknoll: Orbis.
McCartney, Dan. 2009. *James*. Baker Exegetical Commentary on the New Testament. Grand Rapids: Baker Academic.
McKnight, Scot. 2011. *The Letter of James*. New International Commentary on the New Testament. Grand Rapids: Eerdmans.
Moo, Douglas J. 2000. *The Letter of James*. The Pillar New Testament Commentary. Grand Rapids: Eerdmans.
Moore-Keish, Martha L. 2019. *James. Belief: A Theological Commentary on the Bible*. Louisville: Westminster John Knox.
Morales, Nelson R. 2018. *Poor and Rich in James: A Relevance Theory Approach to James's Use of the Old Testament*. Bulletin for Biblical Research Supplements. University Park: Eisenbrauns.
Painter, John. 2004. *Just James: The Brother of Jesus in History and Tradition*. 2nd ed. Studies on Personalities of the New Testament. Columbia: University of South Carolina Press.
———. 2019. "James 'the Brother of the Lord' and the Epistle of James." In *Reading the Epistle of James: A Resource for Students*, edited by Eric F. Mason and Darian R. Lockett, 231–51. Atlanta: Society of Biblical Literature.
Pearlstein, Steven. 2019. "Top CEOs Are Reclaiming Legitimacy by Advancing a Vision of What's Good for America." *Washington Post*, Aug. 19. https://www.washingtonpost.com/business/2019/08/19/top-ceos-are-reclaiming-legitimacy-by-advancing-vision-whats-good-america.
Penner, Todd C. 1996. *The Epistle of James and Eschatology: Re-Reading an Ancient Christian Letter*. Journal for the Study of the New Testament 121. Sheffield: Sheffield Academic.
Perkins, Pheme. 1995. *First and Second Peter, James, and Jude*. Interpretation. Louisville: Westminster John Knox.
Philo. 1993. *The Works of Philo: Complete and Unabridged*. Translated by Charles Duke Yonge. Peabody: Hendrickson.
Ramelli, Ilaria. 2009. *Hierocles the Stoic: Elements of Ethics, Fragments and Excerpts*. Atlanta: Society of Biblical Literature.
Richter, Sandra L. 2020. *Stewards of Eden: What Scripture Says about the Environment and Why It Matters*. Downers Grove: InterVarsity.
Tamez, Elsa. 2002. *The Scandalous Message of James: Faith without Works Is Dead*. Rev. ed. New York: Crossroad.
Tollefson, Kenneth D. 1997. "The Epistle of James as Dialectical Discourse." *Biblical Theology Bulletin* 21:62–69.
Verseput, Donald. 2000. "Genre and Story: The Community Setting of the Epistle of James." *Catholic Biblical Quarterly* 62:96–110.
Vlachos, Chris A. 2013. *James: Exegetical Guide to the Greek New Testament*. Exegetical Guide to the Greek New Testament. Nashville: Broadman & Holman.
Wagner, J. R. 2000. "Piety, Jewish." In *Dictionary of New Testament Background*, edited by Craig A. Evans and Stanley E. Porter, 800. Downers Grove: InterVarsity.
Walker, D. D. 2000. "Benefactor." *Dictionary of New Testament Background*, edited by Craig A. Evans and Stanley E. Porter, 158. Downers Grove: InterVarsity.
Wall, Robert W. 1997. *Community of the Wise: The Letter of James*. New Testament in Context. Valley Forge: Trinity International.

Bibliography

Whitlark, Jason A. 2010. "Ἔμφυτος Λόγος: A New Covenant Motif in the Letter of James." *Horizons in Biblical Theology* 32:144–65.
Witherington, Ben. 1994. *Jesus the Sage: The Pilgrimage of Wisdom*. Minneapolis: Fortress.
———. 2016. *New Testament Theology and Ethics*. Downers Grove: InterVarsity.
Wright, John Randolph. 2023. "The 'Unfading Crown of Glory' as Conceptual Key: Subverting Honorifics in 1 Peter." *Novum Testamentum* 65:83–108.
Wright, N. T. 2011. *The Early Christian Letters for Everyone: James, Peter, John, and Judah*. Louisville: Westminster John Knox.
Wright, Wilmer Cave. 1913. *The Works of the Emperor Julian*. Vol. 2. Cambridge: Harvard University Press.

AUTHOR INDEX

Adamson, James B., 92
Allison, Dale C., 21, 59, 61, 67, 70n95, 74, 80

Barclay, John M. G., 33
Batten, Alicia J., 98, 114
Bauckham, Richard, 10, 37, 113, 117, 126
Bonhoeffer, Dietrich, 134, 138
Bowden, Andrew, 17
Boyce, James L., 39

Calvin, John, 28
Coker, K. Jason, 51, 113

Davids, Peter H., 17n8, 60, 120, 124
Dibelius, Martin, 92, 122–23

Hartin, P. J., 10, 18, 81

Johnson, Luke Timothy, 3, 14n3, 74–75, 90, 103, 110, 120, 125

Kamell, Mariam, 112

Keener, Craig S., 96

Levenson, Jon D., 72

Martin, Ralph P., 42
Maynard-Reid, Pedrito U., 115
McCartney, Dan, 10
McKnight, Scot, 10, 30, 38, 43, 60–61, 66–67, 81, 86, 106, 133–34
Moo, Douglas J., 62, 79–80, 86, 116, 122, 131
Moore-Keish, Martha L., 22, 30, 38, 91, 134, 138

Pearlstein, Steven, 112
Perkins, Pheme, 19

Tamez, Elsa, 53–54, 77

Vlachos, Chris A., 73

Wall, Robert W., 35

SCRIPTURE INDEX

GENESIS

3	30
15	74–76
18	75
22	76
1:26	86
1:28	35
2:2	71
3:6	30
15:6	74–75
22:1–2	28
22:13–18	28
22:1	29
22:2	72

EXODUS

19–24	31
2:23	122
20:6	61
20:13	60
20:14	60
34:6	118, 125

LEVITICUS

5:5	133
16:4	104
16:21	134
16:30	104
19:9–10	52
19:11–13	127
19:15–18	105
19:15	51–52, 59
19:18	59, 106
25:35–36	52

DEUTERONOMY

5:10	61
6:4–5	106
6:5	70
11:14	119

JOSHUA

2:1–24	76
2:11	76
6:22–25	76

1 SAMUEL

4:4	55

1 KINGS

17–18	134

Scripture Index

1 CHRONICLES

17:7	12

2 CHRONICLES

18:26	123

NEHEMIAH

10:29	

JOB

	124
40–42	124

PSALMS

1:6	21
7:17	130
9:2	130
9:7–11	55
9:8–9	55
12	82
12:6	17
13:6	130
17:6	130
21:13	130
24:3–4	104
33:1–3	130
35	130
37, LXX	104
37:7, LXX	104
37:10, LXX	104
38	104
38:6	104
38:9	104
68:3	45
119:43	35

PROVERBS

3:27–28	102
3:30	102
3:31–33	102
3:34	102
4:11	21
4:14	21
5	29
7	29
8:7	35
10:12	138
16:32	38
18:13	38
18:21	86
23:10	45
23:11	46
27:21	17
29:20	37

ECCLESIASTES

12:10	

ISAIAH

1:18	109
3:16–26	104
4:3–4	27
5:8–9	115
6:1	55
10:2	46
13:6	114
40:6b–8	25
45:19	35
58:6	66
61	53

JEREMIAH

5:28	46

Scripture Index

9:23–24	24
13:17	123
14:1–11	104
20:1–2	123
38:1–6	123
48:20	114

EZEKIEL

18:5–9	67
22:7	46

Hosea

4:1–2	97
7:14	114
13:3	110

JOEL

2:23–24	119

AMOS

8:4–6	58
8:8	104

ZECHARIAH

13:9	27

MALACHI

3:1–5	27

MATTHEW

2:14	133
4:21	2
5:3–11	55
5:9	93
5:12	123
5:17	42, 58
5:21–26	86
5:21–22	60
5:34–37	126
5:33–37	127
5:43–44	59
6:19–21	114
7:1	105
8:14–15	133
9:7	133
9:21–22	132
10:2	2
10:3	2
10:8	132–33
10:17	51
10:28	84
12:46–50	4
13:55	2, 4
15:18	45
16:21	133
17:1	2
19:28	7
22:37–40	59
23:29–39	123
24:27	119
24:36	119

MARK

6:3	4
6:13	131
9:23–24	23
9:43	84
11:23	21
12:1	123
12:28–34	67
12:28–32	106
15:40	2

Scripture Index

LUKE

1:46–55	43
1:52–53	26
1:53	53
4:18	53
4:40	132
5:17–26	133
6:20–26	55
6:20–21	26
6:20	52
6:36	125
6:45	45
10:25–37	59
14:13	53
16:19–31	68
21:1–4	53
22:15	29
22:20	31

JOHN

9:2	133

ACTS

1:13	2
1:14	5
2:1–4	83
6	77
7	7
9:36–42	77
12:2	2
12:17	5
14:23	131
15	4
15:1–35	5
15:2	131
22:19	51

ROMANS

1:1	13
3:23–26	74
4:1–5	69
5:3–4	18
5:9–10	132
5:13	30
6:4	133
9:29	115
12–13	69

1 CORINTHIANS

1:31	82
3:10–15	129
5:2	104
12:28	79
15:7	5
15:20–22	133

2 CORINTHIANS

11:24	51

GALATIANS

2	69
2:9–10	4
2:9	5
2:16a	68

EPHESIANS

1:13	35
2:8–9	43, 68
2:10	44, 69
4:11	79

PHILIPPIANS

1:23	29

COLOSSIANS

1:5–6	35
1:5	35
3:12	40

1 THESSALONIANS

2:17	29
3:13	120
4–5	69
5:23	119

1 TIMOTHY

5:17	

TITUS

3:2	40

HEBREWS

5:8–9	20

JAMES

1	61, 97
1:1	12, 126, 9
1:2–18	14
1:2–12	29
1:2–8	137
1:2–4	16, 19, 26–27, 33, 82
1:2	16, 23
1:4	18, 19
1:5–6	45, 132
1:5	19, 22, 32, 83, 89, 97, 102, 111
1:6–8	33
1:6	21
1:7–8	14, 86
1:7	21, 86
1:8	21, 85–86, 89
1:9–11	23, 109
1:9–10	113
1:9	16, 24, 130
1:10	16, 24, 110
1:11	33
1:12–15	26, 33
1:12	16, 26–27, 43, 103, 124
1:13–18	82
1:13–15	28, 43
1:13	16, 28, 32, 83
1:14–15	29, 33–34, 38, 111
1:14	16
1:16–18	32
1:16	28, 67, 137
1:17–18	39, 91
1:17	20, 89
1:18	34, 43, 68, 73, 91, 106, 137
1:19–25	37
1:19–20	43, 79
1:19	32, 37, 45, 67–68, 88, 122
1:20	89
1:21	43, 68, 73, 89, 106, 137
1:22–25	41
1:22	41, 68
1:25	32, 41, 43, 59, 61, 124
1:26–27	45
1:26	16, 79, 81, 104
1:27	68, 92, 111, 120, 129
2	53, 61, 77–78
2:1–13	26, 49, 50, 51, 62, 65
2:1–8	130
2:1–7	58
2:1–4	45, 49–50, 109
2:1	50, 67, 111, 125–26, 132
2:2–5	83
2:2–3	50

Scripture Index

2:2	39	3:9–10	81
2:4	86, 122	3:9	86, 111
2:5–7	49, 52	3:10	86
2:5	32, 54, 107	3:11	89
2:6–7	24, 57, 113	3:13–18	20, 45, 89, 95–96, 98
2:8–9	30	3:13	40, 90
2:8–12	58	3:14	90, 104–5
2:8–11	49	3:15	85, 91, 103
2:8	28, 58, 106, 111	3:16	89, 91
2:9	58–59, 61	3:17	90, 92, 110, 122
2:10–11	30, 62	3:18	43
2:11	30	4	92, 97, 109
2:12–13	30, 49	4:1–12	95
2:12	62, 79	4:1–3	95, 102, 130
2:13	93	4:1–2	122
2:14–26	64–65, 79	4:1	96, 105, 111
2:14–17	65–68, 70, 83, 132	4:2	105
2:14–16	102, 109	4:3	105
2:14	66, 74, 89	4:4–6	95
2:15–16	60, 66–67, 111	4:4	46, 60, 75, 98, 103, 122
2:17	66	4:5	98–100
2:18–19	65, 70	4:6	103, 109
2:18	66	4:7–10	54, 95, 102, 105–6
2:19	9	4:7	85, 104–5
2:20–25	65, 71	4:8	104
2:20	66	4:9	104, 113
2:21	73	4:10	23, 110
2:22–24	73	4:11–12	61, 95–96, 122
2:22	66	4:11	42, 105, 125
2:23	75, 89	4:12	122
2:24	66, 73	4:13–5:12	108
2:25	73, 76, 98	4:13–17	16, 108–9, 111
2:26	66, 93	4:13	110, 112
3	78, 87	4:15	110
3:1–12	45, 78	4:16	110–11
3:1	89, 125	5	109
3:2–3	81	5:1–6	24, 38, 50, 56, 77, 108–9, 112–13, 117, 121
3:2	81		
3:5–6	16	5:3–4	114
3:5	109	5:4	113, 115
3:6–12	83	5:5	104
3:7–8	85	5:6	60
3:8	89	5:7–12	108–9, 118, 123, 125
3:9–12	85	5:8	120

5:9	61, 121	**1 PETER**	
5:10	130		
5:11	118	1:6	17
5:12	125–27		
5:13–20	126		
5:13–18	125, 130	**2 PETER**	
5:13	134		
5:14–16	131	1:1	13
5:14	16, 130, 132, 134		
5:15	133–134	**REVELATION**	
5:17	134		
5:19–20	137–38	7:4–8	7
5:19	91		

www.ingramcontent.com/pod-product-compliance
Lightning Source LLC
Chambersburg PA
CBHW031456160426
43195CB00010BB/996